In short; I love it! It is very concise and to the point; entertaining while at the same time taking you through a series of buildings block relevant to "true Leadership". As an executive and leader in many situation (business or private); I can identify with the context (positive or negative) to either reinforce the positive and continue to work out the negative. I will definitely recom̃ṃẽñd it to you my friends, peers and employees.

Ivan Gorgeon
General Manager
RB Communications, Inc.

Everything in this book made a lot of sense and I truly believe anyone looking to be successful or a leader within themselves or their environment would benefit from reading this.

Scott Hochstadt
President-Starz Lacrosse
CEO Adrenaline Sports
Director-Starz Foundation

This book is very engaging. The examples are both interesting and relevant and appropriate for any experience level. I felt that the book outlined in good balance both the personal and professional qualities necessary for mapping a path to effective leadership. Each chapter builds on the next creating a clear understanding of the interdependencies of the qualities. I also felt the book was tight in its messaging and not fall into the trap of over selling its messages. The authors personality also comes out in the pages which enhances the reading experience.

Luke Dallafior
VP Security Deliver and Business Continuity
British Telecom

"This book is a MUST read for anyone aspiring to become a great leader. It is easy to read and provides some great, real life stories that illustrate the key concepts. Having spent 25 years in the corporate world, it reflected what I had observed."

Jerry Packer, Founder, Executive Financial Services, Inc. and Clean Energy Consultants LLC

I very much enjoyed reading the manuscript. I found it readable and engaging. I wish your thoughts and your teachings could be implemented at a snap of the fingers…they are simply exactly on point. Your work is a manifestation of who you are and your heartfelt opinions how leadership is best conveyed and instilled.

Paul Galleberg
Chief Operating Officer
iCrete, LLC

The book presents an easy to read system of leadership skills on how to become a true leader.

A well organized leadership prescription for both current and new leaders

The book enables the reader to both understand their current leadership strengths and recognize the skills that need to be improved to become a true leader

The author uses a pragmatic style that presents real world examples of leaders using both good and bad leadership skills

The book's examples provide the reader a method to easily access their current leadership experiences.

Roger Benson
Retired, Ex Xerox Senior Director U.S. Sales

A True Leader has Presence is easy to read, yet comprehensive in covering the topic. Ken's use of personal stories gives the reader something tangible to experience and makes what he is sharing more interesting. The book deals with the reality of being a leader, rather than being just an academic review.

Kent Lowell
CEO
Aegeon Corporation

The highest praise I can give is that after several pages, I was caught up in the message. This book will be very valuable to those already ensconced in their management positions and those looking to move upward and forward in their careers. You have an easy style to your writing that keeps the reader from being daunted by the weight of the information. Nicely done.

Janet Singleton.
Real Estate VP
The D.J. Robbins Company, Inc.

A True Leader Has
Presence

The Six Building Blocks To Presence

Kenny Felderstein

iUniverse, Inc.
New York   Bloomington

A True Leader Has Presence
The Six Building Blocks To Presence

iUniverse books may be ordered through booksellers or by contacting:

iUniverse
1663 Liberty Drive
Bloomington, IN 47403
www.iuniverse.com
1-800-Authors (1-800-288-4677)

ISBN: 978-1-4502-4519-7 (pbk)
ISBN: 978-1-4502-4520-3 (ebk)

Printed in the United States of America

iUniverse rev. date: 7/26/10

Thanks

To everyone I interacted with my entire career and life who gave me the knowledge and insight necessary to create this book

To my Ellen who makes me feel mighty — mighty real

FROM THE AUTHOR

Some people and some books claim that leaders are born not created. I don't buy that — completely. Leadership is not built into your DNA. However, aspects of your personality are part of your chromosome string. Personality is one of many elements in the development of presence. It's my contention and the subject of this book that *presence* is the driving force behind leadership. Therefore I believe DNA does play a role, but only one small role.

My parents were working people. Neither one became a manager, director, vice president — leader. As a matter of fact, nobody on either side of my family ever became a leader of any department, company or country. I can only assume my development as a leader didn't come solely from DNA unless my parents were really not my parents or I am an evolutionary mutation. On the other hand, I did get my outgoing personality from my mother and my intellect and drive to get it right from my father. So I guess they were my parents after all and they did have something to do with me becoming a leader.

As a kid I was very popular. I was involved in many team sports and was a great team player. I gave my full support to the team leader. My father owned a very small hamburger joint. I started working there at the age of ten. At thirteen I had a father and son talk with my father, however, I played the role of the father. I spoke — he listened. I suggested ways to improve his business and at the same time reduce the number of hours he had to work. He trusted and respected me. He implemented my suggestions. His life got better.

At thirteen I was managing my father, my mother (who also worked in the store) and one part time person. None of them called me boss and I didn't act like the boss. As far as I was concerned my father was the owner and thus the boss. He paid me my dollar a week and I respected him as my leader. From my perch on the business high-archival limb he had the responsibility to either manage or appoint a manager of the store. He appointed me. As the appointed manager I delegated to the workers. My father chose to play the worker role. Was he a leader? Not in the true sense, but as the owner he got to choose my role and his.

After high school I enrolled in a technical school and majored in computer programming. Computers were new back in 1963. Although I was a poor student in high school, I was a star in computer programming. After six months I was a better programmer than the teacher. He came to me and asked if I wanted to teach the class with him. He said my knowledge was only part of his rationale. The real reason he wanted me to teach was because the students were already using me as their mentor and looked at me as their leader.

I was not trying to usurp my teacher's authority and he didn't accuse me of such. I didn't announce or present myself as the new leader. Hell, I didn't even know I was being looked upon as the leader. Was this happening because I was smarter than everyone else? No! In fact, after teaching for a few months two of the students became much better programmers than I.

After technical school I became a computer programmer at Richardson Merrell Corporation. You probably know them as the company that makes Vicks Vapor Rub. I loved programming. It was my form of art. Nine months later they promoted me to manager of computer services. Today we call that position Information Technology (IT) Manager.

I took the job because it paid more money — bad idea. I was twenty years old and scared to death. I had seven direct reports. The youngest one was six years my senior. On my first day as manager, all seven lined up outside my office waiting to speak to me. Each one had the same words, "I don't know how or why you got this job, but one thing is for sure, I deserve it more than you."

I took this leadership job for the wrong reason. I didn't want to lead. I just wanted more money. Instead of being a programming producer, I became a parent. Instead of doing what I absolutely loved, I found myself managing people that wanted me to fail. The stress and the lack of fun were not worth the few dollars more a week.

I learned a lot about managing and about myself from that experience. I learned the joy of accomplishing a business goal with others. I learned to appreciate the happiness I received from watching my people learn and grow. Having an employee thank me for helping him or her achieve their aspirations gave me a better feeling than any promotion or salary increase I ever received. I never accepted a promotion again for money, ego or power.

I realized that I had to quickly learn how to become an effective manager. In the months that passed my team became *one*. They began to see me as their leader not because I ruled with an iron fist, but because they sensed I was different. With my help two of my team members went on to become department leaders. One of them replaced me when I was promoted.

I have been in leadership roles my entire career. My resume reads; manager, director, vice president, and president — not in that order. I have lead as few as two people and as many as two hundred. I have never asked for a promotion and I have turned a few down. I didn't focus on title, number of people or size of budget. I was the president of a small company and then moved on to a director's job. I was a business unit director and took a job as a marketing manager because I wanted to get back into marketing. A year later I was promoted to director and then vice president. The only common thread throughout my career is that every job involved learning, growing and leadership.

A few years ago I began to wonder, "Why me." I started to look at others to try to determine what traits they had that made them successful leaders. I began to study people that didn't have leadership titles and yet the people around them treated them as their leader. I looked at children, young adults, adults and seniors. Whenever I entered a room with a group of people I would try to pick the one that had leadership written all over them. I was successful more times than not. I would approach those people and ask what they did for a living only to find they were CEOs, directors, team leaders, community leaders, etc. It wasn't just luck. These people had something that stood out.

I have now determined that something is ***presence***.

When I sat down to write this book the first thing I did was go to the dictionary and the web to find the definition of presence. To my surprise, there were many more than I thought. Below is a list of just a few:

- The immediate proximity of someone or something, "she blushed in his presence," "he sensed the presence of danger," "he was well behaved in front of company."

- A control on a guitar amplifier that boosts the upper frequencies above the normal treble control range for added high-end.

- An extra EQ control that allows you to cut or boost the very highest frequencies (above the range of the treble controls).

- The act of being present.

- State of being at a specific place, as in, "Your presence is requested at the wedding of our daughter."

None of the definitions above stated what I am trying to get across in this book. The definitions I found to be associated with what you're about to read are:

- Subjective attitude in which people address one another, respecting mutual humanity and one another's presence.

- Crisp awareness of one's current process, willingness to be met, known, and affected.

- Is the subjective measure of a person's emotional sense that they are part of an environment — that he or she are in the environment's domain or space.

- Appreciation for the experience of another and acceptance of their way of meeting.

- Objective attitude in which a person utilizes executive functions in the pursuit of goals and maintaining concern for outcomes.

- The personal nature of Absolute Consciousness, separated from its own Substance, and is experientially resonantly knowable as a personal environment.

- An invisible spiritual being felt to be nearby.

- Existence, as opposed to non-existence. Presence is the "What Is" -- raw existence of something on a metaphysical level.

Some of these definitions are *way* out there. Some of them I have no clue what they mean — they just sound like they belong. I like my definition best:

Presence, as depicted in this book is, "Something the person who has it knows they have it deep inside their being. The person who is in the presence (the other definition) of someone who has it can *sense* the presence in that individual."

Kenny Felderstein

CONTENTS

FOREWORD

Did you ever play a sport and could tell almost immediately who was the leader of the team? Was that leader the coach?

Did you ever go to a party or join a group and could tell almost immediately who was the leader of the group? Was he or she the life of the party or the designated group leader?

Did you ever join a new department in your company and could tell almost immediately who was the leader of the department? Was that leader the department head?

The answer to the first question in each paragraph is usually yes. The answer to the second question in each paragraph is many times no.

How could it be that the identified leader might not be the coach, group leader or the department head? The answer is that *"A True Leader Has Presence"* — not who has the big stick or title of authority.

When you were growing up you probably encountered bullies that led their clan. Some of these bullies led by being the physically toughest in the group and ruled by force. The leadership tenure of those bullies was usually short because someone tougher always showed up.

Some bullies were not the most physical. They controlled the clan through intelligence and presence. They were true leaders, but were classified as bullies because of the way they asserted their leadership control on others.

Leaders have to get an understanding of what result the people they lead want to achieve. The larger the group the harder it is to meet everyone's objectives. Therefore, true leaders either find a common ground among the people they lead or the leader is able to convince everyone that his result will meet their objectives. Presence is important in reaching common ground. Presence is mandatory if the leader is going to convince the people that the result will meet everyone's objectives.

I am sure that Jim Jones didn't ask each individual if they wanted to drink the lethal Kool-Aid. What Jim Jones did was convince all of the people he led that dying was the objective they all wanted.

True leaders aren't always good guys. Sometimes great leaders have psychotic objectives. Sometimes these true leaders are able to find people that are so unhappy with life or so hungry for power they are willing to follow a psychopath. Can you spell H I T L E R?

The past and the present have evil leaders who use their greatness to repress and destroy. The past and the present also have leaders who use their greatness to enlighten and build. The fine line between the two is defined by the application of their presence. Can you spell **J F K.**

The objective of this book is to identify the building blocks that create presence and how you can make them your own.

Why Do You Want To Become a Leader?

Not everyone upon taking their first breath is destined for leadership. If you want to be a leader for the wrong reasons the burdens you will encounter will quickly overwhelm any of the positives you hope to achieve. When these burdens of leadership overcome the positive return, your days as a leader are numbered.

For many, stepping down is a great relief. No longer pressured by the responsibility of leadership the smart ones go on to much happier lives. However, history has shown that when some leaders see their status slipping away they will do everything in their power to hold on to the tarnished brass ring.

What are the *right* reasons to seek leadership and what are the *wrong* reasons? It's a very complex question to answer. Every individual is different. What could be a right reason for some might be a wrong reason for others. Below is my list. It represents my values. It doesn't mean that if your values are different you will not become an effective leader.

Kenny's Wrong Reasons

- The power to control people.

- More money or other material things mandatory for you to obtain happiness.

- Enhance your ego so others (friends, family, etc.) will love and respect you.

Kenny's Right Reasons

- The belief that you are the best person to achieve your group, company or country's hopes, dreams and desires.

- The opportunity to help the people you lead accomplish their goals and achieve ones they never knew were attainable.

- The opportunity to create a teamwork environment.

- The chance to test and maybe even stretch your capability as a decision maker and influencer of others.

- The opportunity to increase your knowledge of people and life.

- The *preference* of making a happier life for yourself and your family by the additional money and the influence that leadership offers.

This last bullet may sound contradictory to Kenny's Wrong Reasons, but there is a difference between being addicted to power, money and ego versus preferring those things for your happiness and the happiness of the people you care about. An addiction will never be fulfilled. You will just keep seeking more and more. You will lose your focus on achieving happiness and focus only on more power, more money and more ego. It's always good to prefer to have something. However, if you're willing to trade your happiness in order to achieve what you seek, you have become addicted.

Happiness is the forgotten objective of life. We want happiness for our children, family, and friends. However, somewhere along the time line of life we forgot to focus on *our* happiness. We think if we get more money and other material things we will be happy. We think if we become powerful or take a position of leadership we will be happy.

If these beliefs are true then why are so many rich and powerful people unhappy? Why are drug companies selling billions of dollars of anti-anxiety and anti-depression drugs? Why are so many successful people alcoholics and drug users? Why are clinics, therapists, psychologists, psychiatrists and marriage counselors raking in the dough from so called successful people?

The answer is simple, people have lost sight of their true goal — happiness. Companies need true leaders. The world needs great leaders. If you can achieve happiness by becoming a true leader, go for it. If you can achieve happiness by being a productive human being that follows, but never leads — don't rule it out.

THE SIX BUILDING BLOCKS TO PRESENCE ARE ACHIEVED THROUGH:

- **Knowledge**
- **Strategic Thinking**
- **Confidence**
- **Communication**
- **Personal Presentation**
- **Leadership Traits**

By now, I hope you have an understanding of what I mean by presence and why it's important in becoming a true leader. Being able to create a presence requires these two types of capabilities:

- Capabilities you *can not* control (DNA and growing up in a "presence" environment).

- Capabilities you *can* control.

The Building Blocks that follow discuss the ones you *can* control. If you master these building blocks you should be able to overcome any of the missing capabilities you can't control.

The first building block is Knowledge. Strategic Thinking requires Knowledge. Confidence requires Knowledge and Strategic Thinking. Communication requires Knowledge, Strategic Thinking and Confidence. Personal Presentation requires Knowledge, Strategic Thinking, Confidence and Communication. Finally, excellent Leadership Traits are required to become a true leader.

The building blocks stated below come from my years of working on my leadership traits and watching and experiencing presence from the true leaders I have met, worked for or worked with. If you have one of these building blocks you will obtain some presence. If you have all of these building blocks and a little DNA you will be a true leader with a strong presence.

BUILDING BLOCK ONE
KNOWLEDGE

Knowledge is achieved through:

- Life experiences

- Making mistakes

- Focus on what is working — not what is not working

- Appreciation

- Spontaneity

- Listening

- Smart Vs Bright

The saying, "Knowledge is king" is more right than wrong. What is important to people who want to become true leaders is that knowledge enhances presence.

Life Experiences

Just going through the motions of life will not give you the life experiences you will need to create presence. Just reading about life will not work either. Life experiences come from living life to the fullest.

To create presence you have to attack life. That means many things. I am going to discuss a lot of them and I hope you will have done or are going to do more.

Meeting new people will enhance your life experience. This is especially true if the people you meet are from different cultures, different countries, different ethnic groups and different gender groups. These are the people you're going to lead in business or your community. Leaders who are multilingual have more presence than leaders who only speak one language. Leaders that have a real knowledge and understanding of people will have additional presence over leaders that don't.

Life experiences come from trying new things. My parents were the antithesis of this concept. When they went to eat Chinese food every Friday night, they would both order the same thing — shrimps in lobster sauce. Why, because it was a safe thing to order. They had it before and it tasted good. Why change a good thing.

Once a year we went to Atlantic City an hour away from home. We stayed at the same motel, ate the same food and visited the same sites. Only once in the nineteen years I lived at home did we travel somewhere else. That was New York City which was an hour and a half away from home.

We were a very low income family. However, financial problems were not the main obstacle. My parents didn't attack life. Trying new things might not work out so they didn't do it. Status quo was their way of life. Stepping outside their "box" was too scary.

There were many different restaurants where we lived. There were even different Chinese restaurants. We could have tried Greek food, Indian food and even pizza. Believe it or not, my parents never went to a pizza shop to eat a great Philadelphia pizza. They didn't even have one delivered.

Within less than three hours from our home we could have visited Pittsburgh, Maryland, Washington DC Virginia, etc. Each of these cities and states has different kinds of food. They also have people with different points of view about this country, their family and their politics. The history of each of these states is remarkably different. My parents and especially my sister and I would have received many more life experiences if we could have gone to these cities and states instead of Atlantic City every year. Obliviously, I didn't get my presence from my parents' life experiences.

Trying new things is not just about new states, people and restaurants. How about trying new relationships? Marrying your school sweetheart and then having children soon thereafter is not high on my life experience list. Multiple relationships, before you settle down, broadens your life experience and therefore your presence. It could also make you a better spouse and parent when you are ready. Having relationships with people of different religious faiths and different cultures will enhance you life experience even more.

Many of my vacations were spent outside the United States. My wife and I planned enough days so we could experience the country and the people. In my thirteen years at Infonet Services Corporation, Ellen and I had the fabulous opportunity to travel the globe and for six months live in Europe.

If you have the opportunity to visit or live in another country don't stay at an American Hotel with mostly other Americans. Staying at a place where the surroundings look American and everyone speaks English is less scary, but the life experience you will gain is zilch. You might as well travel an hour from your home and stay at a Marriott.

Instead, stay at a local in-country hotel where the patrons are multi-national. At first it will be a little uncomfortable because not everyone will speak your language. However, after a day you will get the hang of it. Through your broken Italian or their broken English you will be able to communicate. The life experience you will gain by communicating with the locals and people from other countries is amazing.

Taking different or new jobs is also important to gaining presence. A leader who has been with the same company in the same job for a very long time will have less presence than a leader who has had many life experiences in different jobs and different companies.

In my forty year career I have been a leader in eight different companies and many different jobs within those companies. Four times in my career I have requested and received lower paying and lower titled jobs so I could broaden my experience. I believed that in the long run it would pay off — I was right all four times.

The larger your world of life experience the more *they* will listen to you. The more they listen to you the more presence you have obtained.

Making Mistakes

Making mistakes sucks. Learning from your mistakes creates knowledge. Making mistakes can happen when you take a task you or your team aren't qualified to accomplish or have a difficult time frame to obtain quality results. This can force you or your team to cut corners and not take the time to think everything through. The end result is poor leadership, a frustrated team and unhappy management.

There is no fun for you or your team completing a task with mistakes. As the leader, you have to be strong enough to tell management or higher ups that you will not accept tasks that don't have a reasonable chance of success. You have to be willing to say to management, "If we try to accomplish this task within the time frame requested we will not be able to deliver the necessary quality. Give us three more weeks and we all will be proud of the result." Another way to say the same thing would be, "I understand the pressure on you to get this task completed within the time frame, but you, management nor my team will be happy with a poor quality result."

Lastly, if you strongly believe the result will not be acceptable and your team will be deemed a failure, I would and have said, "If you insist on doing this task within the requested time frame I suggest you get another team to take it on. I don't want to put my team in a position where they will fail because management is insisting on an unrealistic delivery date."

Although you don't want to set your team up for guaranteed failure, don't completely avoid the risk of making a mistake. Playing it safe is not the solution. A true leader believes he will recover if a mistake should happen. Presence comes from gaining knowledge from your mistakes and the confidence in yourself and the team that you will not make the same mistake twice.

Focus On What Is Right

A big part of gaining knowledge is the ability to focus on what is right instead of always looking for something wrong. The perfectionist focuses on finding things wrong with everything. It's OK to have perfection as a goal. However, not appreciating what is right will lose your perception of the bigger picture. You will not gain enough knowledge unless you see both what went right along with what went wrong. Your team will not be having fun if the only thing you tell them is what they did wrong.

As a leader with presence, your first comment to your people should be to emphasize what they did right. That will make it easier for them to listen to you when you tell them what they did wrong.

People look up to leaders who project balance in their thinking and their actions. People look up to leaders who have a positive attitude. If you consider what went right before you look for what went wrong, your people will respect your balanced approach. Don't avoid what went wrong just make sure it's not the only thing you focus upon.

Balance and positive attitude are critical in achieving presence.

Appreciation

Appreciation is one of my favorite things. It creates a happier career and life. So much knowledge can be gained by taking the time to appreciate the world around you. Leaders display presence when others see them as someone that appreciates life.

Appreciating the people, events and the other things you have should be easy. So why do so many people and especially leaders have a problem with it? A leader's life is very busy. There is always something going wrong. Stress is a big part of their day. Having a large number of needs, wants and desires coming from your employees, spouse, family, friends and yourself, leaves little time to smell the roses.

You just have to take the time to do it. It's not hard. It just takes discipline. For example, on your way home from work don't think about what went wrong that day — think about what went right. When you get home and your spouse, family or friends ask you, "How was your day," the first thing out of your mouth should be something positive. If the only positive thing that happened that day was lunch, tell them about the great ham sandwich.

When you lie in bed at night, think about something you appreciate in life. It could be your spouse, it could be the fabulous sunset you experienced on your way home from work or it could be how much you appreciate your life as compared to others less fortunate than you.

Let me tell you a story depicted in a book by Ken Keys Jr. Mister Keys tells a story about a man in Africa being chased by tigers. After running as fast as he can he finds himself at the end of a cliff with the tigers bearing down on him. He sees a vine that leads all the way down from the top of the cliff to the bottom. With the tigers getting close he starts his way down the cliff. When he gets half way down, he looks up only to see the tigers above waiting for him. He looks down and sees more tigers at the base of the cliff waiting for him. Then he looks straight ahead and sees a beautiful strawberry bush growing out of the cliff right in front of him. He eats one of the strawberries and it's the best strawberry he ever had.

I believe Mister Keys is attempting to get us to understand there will always be tigers above and tigers below. What is more important is to appreciate the strawberries right in front of you. Worrying about what might happen when you get down the cliff will stop you from appreciating what is right in front of you. Take the time to enjoy your life's strawberries.

Let me give you a true personal story that happened to me many years ago before I learned the value of appreciation.

I got home late Friday night from a long and no fun business trip. When I went through my mail I had a postcard notice. The card said I had a certified letter that had to be signed for at the Post Office. It was already too late to get to the Post Office.

That night I had a hard time sleeping because all I could think about was what might be in the letter. Was it another charge from my soon to be divorced second wife's lawyer? Was it bad news from the IRS? I came up with ten more unpleasant scenarios.

I went to a great party Saturday night and instead of appreciating good friends, good food and good music; I was far from the life of the party. Sunday was another bad day. Negative energy was with me the whole day.

After a sleepless Sunday night, I woke up early Monday and drove over to the Post Office. I signed for my letter and tore it open immediately. I figured the sooner I got through the pain of the bad news the better.

The letter was from the State of California reminding all home owners and renters they were entitled to limited earthquake insurance through the California Earthquake Association (CEA) — UGH!!.

I allowed myself to have an awful weekend because I was worried about what bad was going to happen to me. I had a choice. I could have assumed the letter was positive news. Maybe I won the ten million dollar Publishers Clearing House Sweepstakes. The second choice I could have taken was the best choice. I could have decided whatever was in the letter was something I couldn't control until Monday morning. I could have enjoyed and appreciated my Saturday and Sunday. I could have said to myself, "If anything happens, good or bad, it won't happen until Monday."

Whatever was going to be in that letter was a Monday thing. I should have appreciated the "strawberries" of Saturday and Sunday. I should have had more positive energy than negative energy. I should have had enough confidence in myself that even if the letter was bad news, I would be able to deal with it — I always had in the past. I should have realized that positive or negative I was going to gain knowledge about the situation and how I would be able to deal with it. This knowledge would help me in the future. This knowledge would go a long way in establishing my presence. At the time this happened, I was a leader. However, I was not a true leader with presence — YET.

Positive energy begets positive energy. Appreciation begets more appreciation. The things you appreciate enhance your knowledge. People will attach themselves to leaders with presence that display positive energy and who appreciate their life.

Spontaneity

Many leaders are control freaks. Being spontaneous is not one of their virtues. Leaders will gain significant knowledge by being spontaneous every once in awhile. Spontaneity can be described by taking your team to an action movie on short or no notice. It can be achieved by telling your spouse, "Pack your bags, we are driving to Las Vegas today." Spontaneity can be acted on by telling your marketing team that each of them have two days to make a call on a customer to learn how they are using the company's products.

December 21, 1988 was the most spontaneous thing I ever did. Upon waking, I called my administrator to find out if I had any critical meetings that day — the answer was no. I then woke Ellen, my girlfriend of four years, and asked her if she wanted to become my third wife — she immediately said YES! We called a few friends and family to see if they were available to meet us at the Los Angeles Courthouse. Four could make it. Our jeweler opened at ten o'clock. I purchased a wedding band for Ellen and we headed to the Courthouse.

At eleven o'clock our friends and family joined us in front of the judge. Judge Ortiz turned to me and said, "Do you" — I said, "YES." He then turned to Ellen and said, "Do you" — she said, "YES." "I now pronounce you husband and wife. You can kiss the bride." The entire ceremony lasted five minutes — just enough time for a few tears from our cousin Barbara. We took pictures outside the judge's chamber which was next to the Department of Motor Vehicles (DMV). Our group wedding picture was in front of a sign stating DMV information in both English and Spanish.

Coming from two failed marriages, I was very nervous. So much so that our cousin, Steve, had to take me to a small newspaper stand and shove a muffin down my throat so I wouldn't pass out.

Based on my past history, the only way I could have married Ellen was to be spontaneous. I learned a lot from the experience. Ellen is the best thing that has ever happened to me. As she likes to say, "Three *is* a charm."

One of the key rules to enable spontaneous actions is to make sure you're in a position to be spontaneous. Every commitment you make reduces your spontaneous options. Getting married, having children, buying a dog, taking a job with long hours, becoming a leader etc, etc and etc, all have an impact on your spontaneity.

Making commitments is important to being respected. Respected leaders have presence. However, be sure you take into account the impact these commitments will have on your spontaneity.

Marriage can be a wonderful thing, but now you have to share. Now you have to consider the other person's desires. Now you have to discuss before you just run off to ski country with the guys. This is why I have a big problem with getting married at a young age (as I did). Spend your early youth single and spontaneous. If you have a girlfriend you love, both of you should stay single and be spontaneous together. Bottom line, make sure you have weighed the plusses and minuses of marriage before you make that commitment. In the case of my first two wives the scales tipped in the wrong direction. When I married Ellen I was forty four and ready to give up some spontaneity to be with the best friend and spouse anyone could ask for.

Children are a blessing. But, now you and your spouse have another person in your life. This makes spontaneity even more difficult. Children are needy. Every decision you make in life has to include any possible effect it might have on the children. You can't spontaneously run off to Las Vegas by yourselves without considering what you're going to do with the children. I'm not a big favorite of having children early in life (again, as I did). Waiting until our late twenties or early thirties would have been a much better choice. Those early years would have let us gain knowledge from the spontaneous things we would have been able to do. I love my children, but it would have been better to have those early spontaneous years, became financially stable and sorted out the problems in our marriage.

Ellen and I love our five year old dog, Zita Zoe. She is worth every little spontaneous sacrifice we have to give up to enjoy her presence. That's right, Zita has a great presence. She is bright. She let's you know what she wants. Looking into her eyes tells you she has a lot going on in there. She adds a lot of love and value to our lives.

If you get a dog because the kids want one or you think it would be cute to have a dog around — think again. Dogs are needier than cats. Before you get one consider the fact that you will be less spontaneous with one than without one. When Ellen and I want to run off on vacation we have to think about what we are going to do with Zita. Therefore, vacations have to be planned not spontaneous.

Being a leader will make you less spontaneous than if you stay being a team member or individual contributor. Being a leader has many benefits. The down side is the people you lead are now your children. They have to be nurtured, trained and looked after.

That is one of the reasons I'm in favor of finding a "go to person" discussed in Building Block Six. Without that person you will always have to be "on call." Vacations have to be planned well in advance. That's why I wrote, "Don't take a leadership job for money, power and/or ego." It's not worth the spontaneity you will be giving up.

One way to be more spontaneous is to stop planning every thing you do down to the minute. When Ellen and I go on vacation we plan where we are going and where we are going to stay. It stops there. We don't know what we want to do once we get there so why plan it before we leave. We wake up in the morning and say, "What do we want to do today." Many times we don't plan more that a few hours at a time. We might miss out on something, but not the fun of being spontaneous. We also have the attitude that if we like where we have been we will come back again and do the things we missed.

One time we went to Hawaii with friends who had every minute of every day planned before they placed one foot on the island. We felt badly about not joining them on many of their planned events, but some of those events were not what we wanted to do at the time they had planned. Our friends saw Hawaii as a one time thing and felt they had to get it all in. We saw Hawaii as a place we might go back to if we think we missed something.

A leader can't always be structured, organized and controlled. A leader can't always be predictable. If the people you lead know exactly what you will do next they will assume your action instead of paying attention to your lead. Keeping them a little on edge is a good thing. You are a more interesting leader if they say, "I wonder what he will ask us to do next." However, people do expect their leader to be a "rock." Therefore, getting too flakey or being perceived as someone who has no direction or strategy, will negatively affect your leadership.

Spontaneity is good for your mental health and feeds your soul. Being spontaneous enhances your knowledge. With that knowledge you gain more presence.

Listening

The better you listen the more knowledge you will gain. "What counts is in the mind of the listener. It doesn't matter what you say — what matters is what they hear." That is one of my few original quotes and comes from a realization I had in my early years of not being a good listener or a good communicator.

Listening takes patience. Listening requires you to be open minded. Listening means you don't shut the speaker out. Listening means you don't finish the sentence for them because you're too impatient and you believe you know what they are going to say next. Listening means you pay attention to all speakers even if you believe they aren't as smart as you. Accept that the least knowledgeable people sometimes say the smartest things and ask challenging questions.

Time is never on our side. It's hard to listen when the speaker is babbling. Try to sift through the babble and get to the good stuff without shutting the speaker out. Ask questions that might lead to the bottom line quicker. Don't say, "Stop talking and tell me what the bottom line is." Instead say, "Your information is interesting, but I'm not sure I'm getting your point."

After you think you know what the person is saying, test for understanding. As I stated, "What counts is what is in the mind of the listener." You're the listener. Therefore, testing for understanding is required because you might hear something different than what the speaker is trying to communicate. The best way to do this is to repeat what you just heard, in your own words, back to the speaker. Then you ask the speaker, "Is that the point you wanted to make?"

Your goal in listening is to find that golden nugget of information you might not have thought of yourself. Every tiny golden nugget is information that will enhance your knowledge.

Smart Vs Bright

My experience in business and life has convinced me that the best leaders are bright versus smart. I'm not saying you can't be a leader if you're smart but not bright. People attract faster to bright people versus smart people. People look up to and recognize the bright people in the group. People don't attract at all to stupid people. Bright and presence go hand and hand.

So, what is the difference between bright and smart? Why is one more easily recognized over the other? Why are people more attracted to one versus the other?

A smart person is someone that when faced with a new situation or new information will take the time to learn from that situation. In time, the new information will be processed and retained for use at a later time. When another situation occurs the learned information will be helpful or maybe even critical. The smart person will use their learned information to solve the issue or make the right decision.

The key words in the paragraph above are "In time," which means over a period of time. The smart person is very good at holding on to this information and using it to lead when the situation presents itself.

A bright person has all the characteristics of the smart person except when faced with a new situation or new information they get it in real time — NOW. The bright person's brain can process the new information in "real time" not "over time." This enables him to use the information immediately. This enables him to instantly set a course or make a decision. It enables him to lead without delay.

The reason people are more attracted to the bright person is because that person "gets it" the second the information is received. The new information or situation doesn't have to be repeated. The bright person sees or hears it once and the light bulb goes on. The people being led can see in the leader's eyes the information is ready to be used. They look for their leader to tell them what to do next.

The people who are led by the smart person are confident their leader will, "in time", get it. They know he or she is smart and will eventually be able to use the new information to lead them. If their leader has the leadership traits discussed in Building Block Six, they will be patient and trust their smart leader will be able to lead them.

If you have two leaders in an organization or group, one smart and the other bright, my experience has shown the group will be more attracted to the bright leader. I believe this has a lot to do with the bright leader having a greater presence.

The more knowledge you have the easier it is to go from a smart person to a bright person. The more knowledge you have the easier it is to go from a leader to a leader with presence.

BUILDING BLOCK TWO
STRATEGIC THINKING

Strategic Thinking is achieved through:

- *Knowledge*
- Sees the train coming
- Sees the world as it could be
- Creates a vision for the organization and individuals
- Sees tomorrow while focusing on today
- Can it be implemented
- Is there a migration path

Knowledge

Strategic thinking is the next stepping stone toward presence. Strategic thinkers are better served when they have *knowledge* of the past and the present. The more technical, political, historical and human experience they have the better strategic thinkers they become. Knowledgeable strategic thinking leaders have more presence.

The self help books tell you to live in the NOW. As an individual, I agree. Worrying about tomorrow will prevent you from having fun today. Remember, the strawberries right in front of you are the sweetest. However, true leaders with presence have to be able to think strategically while they live in the now.

Sees the Train Coming

People expect a leader to either be a strategic thinker or someone who is willing to listen to the strategic thinkers in the group. You can be a good leader if you take strategic inputs from someone else. However, Leaders who think strategically themselves or are able to build on the ideas of someone else, have more presence than leaders who only count on the strategy of others.

To be an excellent strategic thinker you have to be willing to use your quiet time to think about where *this* is all going. You have to be able to see what others can't see. You have to see that train coming and know what to do to get out of the way *before* it hits you.

Strategic thinking requires planning. A true leader should be bright enough to see all the options quickly, but well prepared if they have to make that spur of the moment decision. A leader who has a requirement to get in front of the train should have spent some time thinking about, "What if the train doesn't stop? It's not supposed to happen, but what if it does?" The team expects the leader to have a plan. That strategic plan should have more than one option. I like to call it "Plan B," Plan C" etc.

True leaders do their homework and take the time necessary to think their ideas through. However, all the homework, planning, or quiet time will not guarantee positive results. In the final analysis, the true leaders with presence have to trust their research and their *gut* on the forward strategy they envision.

Sees the World as It Could Be

The statement, "Sees the world as it could be — not just as it is now" is an important aspect of strategic thinking. Steven Jobs is an obvious example. The people at Sony had a strategic thinker who came up with the Walkman. Years after that breakthrough product Sony didn't have the strategic thinking to see the world changing to digital. If they did, they surely didn't understand what going to digital could mean. Steven Jobs understood. He saw a world where people would use computers plus their internet connection to download their content to a digital device. Sony's Walkman required you to buy tapes. Today if you ask many people if they heard of a Walkman, they would say, "No". However, ask almost everybody if they ever heard of the IPod and ITunes you will get a resounding, "YES!"

Mister Jobs also saw computer digital 3D CGI (Computer-Generated Imagery) production's use in making animated movies while Disney was still doing 2D (pen on paper) animated movies. Seeing the world as it could be not as it's now, is why Mister Jobs' companies are thought of as leaders while giant companies like Sony and Disney are not. When a new leader replaced the head of Disney, he appreciated the strategic thinking of Mister Jobs' company PIXAR and purchased it for billions — "If you can't beat them, buy them."

Through out the world we have many examples of leaders with a strong presence who were or are strategic thinkers. Sir Richard Branson sees us traveling outside our atmosphere to get to different places or just enjoy the ride. Steve Wozniak saw people everywhere using a small personal computer. He called it the Apple. Mister Wozniak also created the universal entertainment system remote control.

There are many not so obvious examples happening every minute of every day. A military leader has to be a strategic thinker. A corporate leader has to be a strategic thinker. A group leader has to be a strategic thinker. A community leader has to be a strategic thinker.

Don't you just love true leaders with great presence who are strategic thinkers — I do.

Creates a Vision for the Organization and Individuals

Companies fail to meet their objectives in large part because they don't have a vision of today and where they will be in the future. Departments within the company fail to meet their objectives for the same reason. The result could lead to a significant negative impact on the company's market value.

Below are two examples:

- Apple's President and CEO Steven Jobs believed that for computers to become the mainstay of consumers it had to be smaller and less expensive than corporate computers. He also believed consumer computers had to have an easy to use graphical interface. He had managers who didn't share his vision and just wanted to stay the course on their growing consumer Apple computer. Mister Jobs, being the final decision maker at Apple, let the consumer division do their thing while he himself managed a small group of visionary developers who created the Macintosh (Mac as we call it today).

  A few years later the Mac was a success, but couldn't gain significant market share from lower cost Microsoft based computers. The Apple Board of Directors felt that Mister Jobs couldn't make Apple a major player because he was an engineer not a marketer. Obliviously the Apple Board was wrong and didn't appreciate his vision.

Apple's Board lost Mister Jobs' vision when they replaced him with a marketing person from Pepsi. After years of poor performance the Apple Board brought back Mister Jobs. His first day on the job, he used his vision of Apple today and what it could be in the future to rebuild the failing company.

Mister Jobs pushed his vision down into the organization and got the managers of the various departments to buy into his vision. The managers who could take the vision and get their people to buy in, became leaders. Today, almost every consumer knows Apple and its products. Vision and leadership is the mainstay of Apple today.

Mister Jobs is a leader with great presence who not only uplifted Apple, he also created a significant computer company called NEXT and a major movie production company called PIXAR (the company who created Toy Story, Monsters, Finding Nemo, CARS, Ratatouille, etc.).

- The monopoly protected telephone companies thought they didn't need a vision. They had a cash cow business that was bullet proof. Then competition showed up. Cable companies showed up. The internet showed up. This forced the minute price per call to go down. Almost overnight the telephone companies found themselves in deep do-do.

These events forced the telephone companies to think about and create a vision of what they wanted to be now and in the future. Some have decided to stay the course. Some have decided their best bet is to become a major player in the mobile phone business. In my opinion these limited vision companies will not become the leaders.

The companies I believe will become the leaders are the ones that have decided their vision is to be a multimedia company. In the US, Verizon and AT&T are leading the charge.

Just think about AT&T. They were a telephone monopoly with no need to have a vision. Oops, the government broke them up into little pieces to create competition. When competition arrived they still continued doing business as usual. Finally, when it dawned on them that the prices they must charges for a phone call was coming down to their cost, they decided to think about and create a vision for today and the future. Offering a rich set of features with the phone (voicemail, call forwarding, caller ID, etc.) enabled them to almost give away the call per minute and make a profit on the features.

When the internet and cable companies started using voice over the internet (VOIP), AT&T expanded their vision to become a multimedia company. Adding DSL and other internet services got them into the internet game. The merger with Cingular made them a major player in the mobile phone business. Now they are delivering TV to the home and business. When the national roll-out is complete, a consumer could get all of their voice, video, TV and internet needs from one company.

Cable companies had this vision of the future from the beginning. They knew their large cable bandwidth coming into the home would open the door for them to deliver multimedia services. Their first step was to get the cables into the home with a product everyone needed and wanted — TV service.

Verizon and AT&T didn't have that vision when they built and delivered phone services. Their basic phone service did and still doesn't have the bandwidth to deliver multimedia services.

To implement their vision, leaders at AT&T and Verizon had to get the shareholders to agree to spend a lot of money on this vision. I believe it's in the billions. This was and still is a big risk. It also required leaders at the top to get everyone in management and individual employees to buy into the vision. At Verizon and AT&T this was and is a bigger task than many other companies because of its roots as a laid back telephone monopoly.

You can chastise the phone company's leadership for their lack of early vision. I give them credit for accepting they had to change, convincing Board members to take the risk by investing billions and making culture changes within the company so they can better compete.

No vision — no presence. No presence — no true leadership.

Sees Tomorrow While Focusing on Today

I hope you're not getting the idea that all strategic thinkers are leaders. Many of the best strategic thinkers are either people we never heard of or people we heard of that never led anything. I have had the wonderful opportunity to work with strategic thinkers that saw the world as it could be while sitting in their little cube all day. At Xerox alone, I worked with staffers and leaders that envisioned the first laser printer and the software that created the fonts on the first laser printers. Dr. John E. Warnock, executive leader at the Xerox Palo Alto Research Center left Xerox with that software and formed Adobe Corporation. He called the highly successful software Postscript. Today Postscript is now known as "pdf files" and is one of the standards in the electronic document industry.

Dr. Warnock is a true leader with presence. Xerox let him leave with the software because they didn't have the vision to see Postscript as an industry leader. At Xerox, I was also involved with the staff people who created the computer mouse. These people worked in Dr. Warnock's organization.

Leaders are people that focus on today while they use their quiet time to do their strategic thinking. There are tasks to be worked on today. The leaders of a team, group, company, community or country, have to make sure today's tasks are getting done on time with great quality. The big win comes from a forward strategy that builds upon today's work.

Leaders are people that focus on today while they use their quiet time to do their strategic thinking.

Can It Be Implemented

A true leader has to ask, "Does my future strategy make sense. Would anybody buy it? Can it be implemented? Will others that have to agree, support it? Will it get stopped by politics? Will it get stopped by company policies? Will it get stopped by legal?"

Strategic thinkers come up with all kinds of ideas. The best strategic thinkers can sift through all of their ideas and choose the one(s) that can be implemented. I have witnessed many interesting concepts that couldn't be implemented and therefore die before they get started. Even worse, I have witnessed interesting ideas that die midway through the project after millions of dollars have been spent.

I was involved in such a project at Xerox's Diablo division. Diablo was the leader in dot matrix printers sold into the consumer market. Dot matrix printers came years before consumer laser and ink jet printers.

Xerox's strength at that time was in corporate marketing. They knew nothing about the consumer market. The consumer market was very different than the corporate market. In addition to the size and cost of the product, printers in the consumer market had to be much more reliable. Corporate customers were not as sensitive to the reliability of the Xerox 9700 laser printer because there was a Xerox service person assigned to every corporate account. If the printer went down the repair person fixed it that day. Years ago, Xerox products broke about once every six to eight weeks. Consumers expected their printers to break no more than once every two years.

Delivery time was another difference maker. Xerox products were sold by Xerox sales people directly to the corporation with a four to six week delivery time. Consumer products were sold by stores that expected delivery of no more than a day if they ran out of product. They would lose a sale if the customer had to wait. Today, corporate customers expect reliability and product delivery similar to the consumer market.

Xerox was not equipped to meet both the reliability and the delivery requirements demanded by the consumer market. Their solution was to buy Diablo because of its consumer experience.

A strategic thinker at Canon Corporation sold the company on creating a consumer based copier. The uniqueness of their copier was that it had a replaceable cartridge which held the black electrostatic charged powder (toner) that created the characters on the page. In addition, many of the parts that were needed to print the page were included in the cartridge.

This copier was much more reliable than all other copiers on the market because the user would run out of toner and therefore change the cartridge well before the copier broke. Besides reliability, this new concept had a tremendous feature other copiers didn't — you could sell the copier at slightly above cost because the profit was in selling the cartridges. This "razor — razor blade" approach (sell the razor at cost and make your money on the blades) was a huge profit maker for Canon.

A strategic thinker at Hewlett-Packard (HP) sold the company on creating a consumer laser printer based upon the Conon copier. HP would buy the copier from Canon, add its own electronics and fonts and sell the printer to the same consumer stores it was selling its personal computers. The HP LaserJet was an instant success then and is a huge money maker for HP today.

The HP LaserJet story depicts how strategic thinking along with the capability to implement makes for a great return on profit. It also led to the creation of other strategic ideas that might never have been created if the LaserJet was a flop.

You're probably wondering, "What the hell does this HP story have to do with Xerox and Diablo?" The Xerox Diablo story I'm about to tell you is the antithesis of the HP story and explains why implementation is critical to strategic thinking.

Xerox didn't buy Diablo because it wanted to sell dot matrix printers to consumers. Xerox wanted to have a consumer product that could compete with the HP LaserJet. Xerox believed it had to get into the consumer market for its long term growth.

Two years after the LaserJet's success, a strategic thinker at Diablo sold the company on the idea of using a different technology to get the characters on the page. It was called Ionography. The concept was to use an Ion gun instead of a laser to create the characters. Ionography would be less expensive and more reliable than lasers. Xerox would use the copier from its Fuji Xerox partnership. The Fuji copier was competitive with the

Canon copier and used the cartridge approach. The project code name was Scrapper. As it turned out Scrapper was a more appropriate code name than any of us thought.

Six months into the Scrapper project I was promoted to the marketing team. Five months later and after spending many millions of dollars on starting up and retooling a new manufacturing plant in Japan, I realized the product would never meet the requirements to compete with the LaserJet.

Ionography was a difficult technology to control — lasers were not. The Ion gun has to have a manufacturing tolerance much greater than a laser. That meant producing mass quantities of Scrappers in short periods of time was impossible. The real blow came when I realized this technology would never meet the image quality standards of the LaserJet. I used focus groups of all kinds and the results came back the same every time. Everyone picked the LaserJet over Scrapper in blind tests.

I went to the president of Diablo, put my Xerox badge on the desk in front of him and said that I would not launch Scrapper. I stated that I was aware of the pressure on him to launch the product because of the millions of dollars spent and the need to come up with a LaserJet fighter. However, I reminded him that should we go forward with the launch, Fuji Xerox would have to spend many more millions finishing the new manufacturing plant and delivering Scrappers to the market. Lastly, I strongly made it clear to him that should Scrapper fail in the market, the Xerox brand would suffer by the bad reviews from the media and a whole lot of unhappy customers.

The president was not happy with my feedback. He had two choices. Launch Scrapper no matter what the results or go to the president of Xerox and tell him he wasted millions of dollars. I believe my point about the Xerox brand resulted in his decision. He told me to pick up my badge. Thanked me for my courage and said he would speak to Paul Allaire immediately. After his conversation with Mister Allaire, Scrapper was scrapped.

The strategic idea of using an Ion gun instead of a laser made sense from an economic and reliability point of view. However, when it was discovered early into the testing that the product couldn't be implemented within the marketing requirements, engineering and manufacturing management kept going instead of suggesting a shut down. I spoke to the manufacturing people on the floor and they told me about the problems. When I approached their management, they told me to focus on marketing and let them get their job done. I believe they took this attitude because they knew senior management in both Diablo and Xerox wanted to launch a state of the art product.

This was not good leadership on their part. They could have stopped the Ion project and gone with lasers before many of the millions were spent. Their Ion gun vision was their baby and they didn't want to tell anybody their baby was ugly.

A strategic thinking leader who doesn't take into account the risk of implementation is not only a poor leader he or she will fail in the presence category. This is because people will see them as strategic *wishful* thinkers not leaders who encourage inputs from others even if it means the project might have to be cancelled.

Is There A Migration Path

The strategic thinker sometimes only sees their big idea as a one-off concept. It's others that take that idea and build on it. Great strategic thinkers see their idea as a continuum. The Sony Walkman was a one-off device. It played music. Apple's IPod had a migration path from its onset. It started with music and then migrated to video. Then it migrated to a multimedia device called the IPhone. The IPhone is a phone, camera, music and internet device with downloadable video. Everyone can't wait to see the next migration path — the IPad.

This migration didn't happen by accident. I'm sure it was strategically thought through from the beginning. I would bet Apple has the next ten plus years planned for the IPod/IPhone/IPad. Just to be an "I told you so," in 2011, I expect to see an IPhone/IPad that can do video calling. That's you talking to me while we both can see each other in full motion video.

NOTE: I wrote the last sentence in January 2010. Apple already exceeded my expectations when it launched the new iPhone 4 in June 2010. This new phone has the capability to do video calling. I'm sure we will see an iPad with video calling some time in 2011.

BUILDING BLOCK THREE
CONFIDENCE

Confidence is achieved through:

- *Knowledge*

- *Strategic Thinking*

- Accomplishment

- Making Decisions — Taking Risks

- Fear of Failure

- Responsibility

- Commitment

- Not being defensive

- Figure out how you can — not why you can't

Knowledge and Strategic Thinking

Continuing my building block theme, leaders who have *knowledge* and think strategically have more presence than those who don't. Knowledge makes you feel more confident because you have information to give to others that will enhance their knowledge. Knowledge enables you to understand what others are telling you because you experienced similar situations. The more you understand the more confidence you feel and project.

Strategic thinking gives you confidence. If your ideas are applauded by others and implemented by the team, you will have the confidence to deliver additional concepts. If your strategies are successful, others will have confidence in you which will build more confidence in yourself.

Confidence plays a significant role in presence. People are attracted to people who have confidence. Confident people like being with other confident people. Less confident people want to be associated with confident people because they hope some of it will rub off on them.

Boastful confidence doesn't work. You can say you're confident all you want, but saying it doesn't attract people. People are attracted to internal confidence. They can sense you believe in yourself and the people you lead. They can sense you know deep inside that you and the team will get the task or project done on time with excellent quality.

When a confident person enters a room the people around him or her feel their confidence and therefore feel their presence.

Accomplishment

Having a sense of accomplishment over and over again is a big part of gaining confidence. The people you lead will trust your judgment if they know you have had many accomplishments. The people you lead will strive to complete their tasks if they know that when you're given a task you will somehow find a way to achieve it. Most importantly, the people you lead will see your presence through the eyes of your accomplishments.

To project accomplishment you have to accomplish something — DUH! Is that a stupid statement — NO! There is a method to achieving something. Start with taking a task you have the time and skill to complete. At the beginning, taking a task that is high risk, highly visible and something you have limited skill or time to complete is not a good building block toward accomplishment. Once you have many accomplishments under your belt you can then branch out to the more risky tasks.

When doing these early tasks, make sure you finish them on time or earlier. Also, make sure they are done right with all the "*Is*" dotted and the "*Ts*" crossed. Precision is critical in these early tasks. Being anal about every little detail is a good thing.

When you have accomplished the task, pat yourself on the back. Tell yourself, "good job Kenny." Go to bed that night and appreciate what you have accomplished. Doing these things will build your confidence.

After completing a few of these tasks tell the world. Don't do it after the first one because you will be perceived as a bragger. Some might label you as a one task wonder. However, after a few accomplishments and with the swagger of presence, they will be impressed. When I say, "Tell the world" I mean just that. Tell your team, your management, your management's management, your parents, spouse and friends. Do it in a way so you don't come off as a boaster. Make sure you acknowledge all the other people that helped complete the task.

Accomplishment without anybody knowing about it is like the question, "If a tree falls in the woods and nobody hears it, does it make a sound?" There should not be any doubt in everyone's mind as to who finished these tasks — IT WAS YOU plus the people who helped you. You will never become a leader with a strong presence if you go through life anonymously. "Say it loud — say it proud." After awhile you won't have to be so blunt about telling them. They will assume that when they give you a task it will be accomplished on time and with great quality.

Confidence can come at an early age. If your parents had confidence within themselves, you had a good chance of growing up with some confidence in yourself. If your parents had a positive outlook on life, you had a good chance of growing up with a positive outlook. If your parents let you accomplish tasks on your own, the result of each accomplishment helped build your confidence.

I didn't have such parents. They grew up in the great depression. They had parents from Europe who were poor and had a very pessimistic outlook on life. This created my parents negativism which they gave to my sister and me. My parents lacked confidence in themselves. My father grew up with a dead father and a sickly mother. At eighteen he had to help support his three sisters. He was scared all the time. With the help of others they just about had enough to survive.

My mother grew up in a comparable environment. She was the baby girl with four brothers a sickly father and a mother who didn't speak English. The family loved my mother. However, their love was shown by not letting her do anything on her own for fear she would be disappointed if she failed. My mother didn't accomplish very much which created her lack of confidence.

My parents worked so hard they didn't have a lot of time to focus on my sister and me. Their main goal was to provide for and protect us from the cruel outside world. They worried about us taking on any significant tasks because we might fail. My parents were unhappy because they feared failure. They believed that if we failed we would grow up unhappy. My parents didn't instill confidence in my sister or me.

This lack of confidence and fear of failure had a devastating effect on my sister. She was always unhappy. She needed to have a father who would comfort her, but he couldn't be there for her physically or emotionally. She turned to alcohol in her twenties and spent another twenty years miserable before she went to AA. After ten years of sobriety, she died of cancer.

Somehow I was able to see my parents' fears and realize it was their problem not mine. Even though I had this deep seated fear of failure and lack of confidence inside me, I was motivated to not grow up like them.

Sports were my salvation. At a young age I was a pretty good baseball pitcher and a decent football receiver. I was small in stature, but fast on my feet. I was a great team player and had the same strong work ethic as my father. My parents didn't want me to play sports for fear I would get hurt and might fail. They were right on their first concern. Over my years in baseball and football I tore up my shoulder, broke my ankle in two places, broke a finger and toe and chipped a bone in my skull. Those physical problems were minor compared to the plusses I received from sports. Having many personal and team accomplishments helped me overcome my fears and insecurities. This enabled me to become more confident.

At twenty, I was working in corporate America. My sister played out her lack of accomplishment, lack of confidence and fear of failure by becoming an alcoholic. I played out my fear of failure and lack of confidence by becoming a workaholic.

Workaholic can be as destructive as alcoholism. I did accomplish a lot which enhanced my confidence. However, it cost me a marriage, difficulties with one of my two sons and years of no fun. Over time I was able to balance work, family, friends and fun without losing any confidence. As a matter of fact, I had and have more accomplishments and more confidence as a balanced person than an unbalanced workaholic.

If you didn't grow up as a confident person you can acquire confidence by every small and large accomplishment. Accomplishment begets confidence. Confidence begets presence.

Making Decisions — Taking Risks

A true leader will take calculated risks. Calculated risk taking is different than taking a risk just because you want to impress upper management that you are a risk taker. Taking a risk on a task might lead to making mistakes. True leaders take calculated risks with the confidence that should something go wrong, they and the team will have a "Plan B" and "Plan C" to correct the mistakes and get the task done on time with excellent quality.

Confident people make decisions. I stated in my first book "Never Buy a Hat if Your Feet are Cold — Taking Charge of Your Career and Your

Life," "If you make more right decisions than wrong decisions, you will be successful. No decision is a wrong decision."

The people you lead expect you to make a decision. Just making a decision doesn't mean they will see you as a leader. People want more than decisiveness they want the person making the decision to demonstrate internal confidence that this is the right decision.

Fear of failure stops people from making decisions and taking risks. I stated that people can sense someone's confidence. People can also sense fear of failure. How do you get rid of fear of failure — by being confident! How do you gain confidence — by making decisions and taking calculated risks!

The more decisions you make that turn out right, the more confidence you gain. The more wrong decisions you overcome by having a "Plan B," the more confidence you gain. The more calculated risks you take that turn out right, the more confidence you gain.

Early in my career as a sales technical support person I was faced with a decision that included a calculated risk. My sales manager informed me that a District System Manager's job was open working out of Philadelphia. I wanted the promotion and I also wanted to go back to my home town. I only had one year with the company and even though I had previous management experience the chance of getting the job over more senior people was very small.

In my red VW Karmann Ghia convertible, I made the trip from Rochester New York to the regional sales office in White Plains New York. It was cold and snowy. The roads were slick and I couldn't go very fast. By the time I arrived in White Plains it was twelve thirty at night and I had an eight AM interview with the Regional Sales Manager. I went to the hotel where I had a reservation only to find they gave my room to someone else. I was upset because I forgot to ask for a late arrival. The hotel manager told me about a motel about one mile away that might have an open room.

Visibility was poor and I almost passed the place because only the "O" and the "T" of the MOTEL sign was lit. I went to the small front desk and rang the bell. I asked the older man with a three day beard for a room. As he was speaking to me he kept looking out the front window at my car. I wasn't sure what he was looking for until he asked me how long I was going to stay. I said, "The night." He then said, "You mean the *whole* night." I should have realized then what kind of motel this was, but I was young, exhausted and just wanted to get some sleep.

I arrived at room 104 and let myself in. I was not happy that an old boiler which made a banging noise was next to the room. I flipped on the light switch by the door, but no lights went on. I then felt my way to the bed and turned on the lamp. The lamp had a thirty watt bulb which only lit up a five foot area. I then noticed water was running in the bathroom. I flipped the bathroom light switch — no light. The running water was coming from the sink. I turned the cold water knob to shut off the water, but the handle just spun in my hand with no effect on the running water.

I went back to the office and rang the bell. The older man was not happy to see me. I told him about the problems with my room and his comment was, "Hay buddy, this ain't the Ritz." Room 110 was not any better light wise, but at least I couldn't hear the banging of the boiler and the running of water. I laid my rain coat on the top of the bed and with all my clothes on, I went to sleep.

The next morning I arrived at the Regional office to meet with Terry the Regional Sales Manager. I was in my early twenties and very aggressive. My intense nature helped in some interviews, but in this case being more laid back was a better strategy. Terry was a tall slim soft spoken Englishman. Not much excited him. Fortunately my lack of sleep put me in a relaxed mood.

Terry and I spent an hour together. I thought he was impressed. While we were shaking hands goodbye Terry said, "Kenny, I'm sure you could do a good job as the District Systems Manager however, your competition are the other field systems people with more technical experience and tenure than you. I hope you won't be disappointed if I select one of them over you." My immediate response was, "Terry, if you don't hire me for the job you will be the big loser. My competition might have more technical experience and tenure than I, but I can manage people and tasks. I've been doing it since I was thirteen. Don't hire them because they worked at the company longer. Hire me because I'll fix the problems in Philadelphia and build a cohesive productive systems team."

I then braced myself for Terry's response. The risk was my bold statement might not be received well resulting in a rift between us. Terry said nothing and looked a little shocked as I left the office.

Two weeks later I was wondering if I was going to be fired or hired when Terry called and gave me the good news. He never said it had anything to do with my closing remarks, but my manager told me it did. He told me I was lucky because the risk I took in a political company like Xerox might cost me a job rather than get me a job. I told him that doing the politically correct thing was something I would have to learn because it was not in my nature and definitely not my management style.

Taking a risk and making a decision is hard for many people. Did you ever hear the statement, "I'm so confused?" There is no such thing as being confused. You're really saying you don't want to make a decision because you're afraid you will make the wrong decision. You're not confused. You know what to do. You just aren't sure your decision will turn out right.

In business if you make more right decisions than wrong decisions you will be successful. No decision is a wrong decision. In management, if you will not take a risk how in the world could you ever expect your employees to take any risks? More importantly, "Life without any problems means you haven't taken any risks. Life without risk is half a life."

If you want to be a leader and get a lot out of life you're going to have to consider taking some chances, making some decisions and maybe making some changes. You can not be indecisive. You always have to assess the risks of your decisions. After assessment you can't be on the fence. To take the gamble or not take the gamble is a choice you will have to make.

You will never have presence if you don't show the ability to take chances. Your lack of risk taking will be viewed as a lack of confidence which will show in your eyes and your body language.

Fear Of Failure

Leaders don't fear failure. Leaders assess failure. They watch out for the early signs of failure. If they see it coming they make a new plan and execute their "Plan B." That new plan most likely has a degree of risk associated with it. However, a leader learns from mistakes. Armed with advanced knowledge, the leader sets a new path that has less chance of failure.

"The goal is to, "Maximize your minimum risk."

Why do we all have this risk averting problem? Because that is the way we were brought up. Our parents didn't bring us up to take risks. Why would they? That's not the way their parents raised them. You don't tell a child, "Try crossing the street on your own and see how it goes." It doesn't work that way. A good parent always tells the child, "Be careful, don't do that, watch out for this, let me take you so you won't get hurt."

What message do those protective parent's statements portray to the child? They are telling their children there are consequences if they make the wrong choice. If they fail they could get killed. Parents want to control those risks. Parents want to protect their children. Parents want their children to be happy. Parents want their children to have a long life. Parents want their children to be free of any risk. Some parents are more concerned than others. However, the bottom line is we raise our children to minimize their risk taking and minimize their decision making.

We all have this risk adverting child running around inside of us. Some to a greater degree than others. If you have any chance of becoming a leader with presence you have to overcome your natural propensity to avoid taking chances. This means you have to commit to making a decision, taking a chance, changing a job, getting a divorce, deciding what dinner we are going to eat tonight. It could be a little decision like dinner or it could be a giant decision like divorce. Not making a decision or being unwilling to take a risk doesn't position you as a leader with presence.

This might sound easy — it's not. This little child inside of us pushes back on every decision by saying, "What if I do that and it turns out to be the wrong thing to do. It might backfire. I might make a mistake and oh my, if I do, I might lose my job. If that happens, I will lose my money. If that happens, those who love me will stop loving me and I will be unloved. If that happens, oh crap, I might wind up on the street with no love and no money — I might die."

This little child inside of us can go from making a decision, taking a risk, to death. I'm serious. That is what goes on inside your body and it all came from your upbringing. What if I guarantee you will survive 99.9% of all your business and life decisions? I am also going to guarantee you will always have food to eat, air to breathe and shelter. Everything else is cosmetic. Let me repeat that, "You will always have food to eat, air to breathe and shelter. Everything else, your watches, your rings, your cars, are cosmetic."

How can I guarantee it? How do I know this to be true? If you're reading this book you have an education. You're most likely a legal citizen in your country. Go visit the people in your town that don't have an education and aren't legal citizens. I have and here is what I found. They have food to eat, air to breathe and shelter. They don't have nice cars, new appliances or most of the material things we have. However, they aren't dead. On the contrary, most of them are happy with good families and friends. They scratch by, but they do productive work and contribute to society.

Most likely your decision will enhance your happiness not diminish it. So, make a decision. Take a risk. You will survive and be loved even if you make a bad decision. Leaders make decisions. Leaders take risks. Leaders don't live in fear of failure. Leaders believe that if they make a wrong decision they will find a way to recover. People follow leaders because they believe they will lead them in the right direction. Every decision requires some degree of risk. No risk — no leadership — no presence.

As I stated above, that little child inside of us grew up with fears. Fear they might get hurt, fear they will not make something positive out of life and even fear they might not survive. However, the fear that stops most of us from becoming a leader is the fear of failure.

What is this fear of failure? Fear of failure is not a today thing — it's a tomorrow thing. You're not worried about what is happening now. You're worried about what is going to happen in the future if you take this risk or make this decision or make this change. So you go through life fearing the future not the present. We know what is happening in the present. It's the unknown future that we fear.

In my first book I quoted something from a very talented friend, Mike Bemiss. He called it "Beware of the Known."

"It's not the UNKNOWN we must fear. As children everything was unknown. As we get older we start to build walls around ourselves at the limit of what we KNOW. We build the walls of our own jail with the fear of failing at doing something UNKNOWN.

Too soon we build a castle of security around ourselves. It has no doors and few windows — it's the KNOWN. We live and die in there with only an occasional timid peak out a high window at the UNKNOWN.

We build the walls of our KNOWN so high that we cannot escape and our souls whither and die for lack of new experiences.

I refuse to build that wall. Each stone I would use to build it, I'll use instead as a stepping-stone into a new and different UNKNOWN. When I die, as we all do eventually, my only regret will be that I never got to discover the next UNKNOWN just over the horizon.

I want to build my castle around the entire Universe. I appreciate the KNOWN. But I refuse to be limited by it. The KNOWN can be a trap if you let it and you will never experience the next UNKNOWN which is the most special UNKNOWN of all — the next one."

Responsibility — Accountability

Someone who takes responsibility unto themselves has confidence. "Not my job" — no confidence. "I had nothing to do with that" — no confidence. "I'll do it, but don't blame me if it doesn't work" — no confidence. "I've got this one" — confidence. "Trust me, I'll get this done on time and with good quality" — confidence. Team, don't worry, if anything goes wrong, I'll take the heat" — confidence.

If you truly believe in your ability, your decision making and your capability to overcome problems, you have the confidence that others will sense. If you're afraid of being blamed and if you're afraid to stand up and be counted, you don't have that inner-confidence. Without that inter-confidence you will not be viewed as a true leader with presence.

I like people who are accountable for their own actions. I like people who stand up and say, "I own this task — I will make it happen. If the task fails, blame me. If the task succeeds, applaud the team and me." A leader realizes the buck stops with him or her. If consensus is desired or required, they will make every effort to gain the approval of others. However, even if consensus is reached, leaders know they will be accountable for the final result.

If things go wrong, a true leader never says, "Don't blame me. Everyone agreed to go forward." If things go right, a true leader says, "Yo team, great job — high fives to everyone."

The following is a true story regarding how some so called leaders don't take responsibility for their actions:

I reported to a marketing executive who was *not* leadership material. We were making a product presentation to the CEO of our division. Don and I worked for many days preparing the presentation. I had a problem with statements on two of the slides. I told Don these statements were negative and without a stated recovery plan. I suggested he remove them from the presentation. Don insisted the statements stay in their current form.

I was a good soldier and complied. I was not worried because Don was the executive and he was the one standing up in front of the CEO. The presentation was going great until we got to the eighth slide. One of Don's statements irritated the CEO and he let Don know it. I will never forget the words that came out of Don's mouth. "Bob, I'm sorry about that statement. I told Kenny to take it out, but I guess he forgot."

Others had told me that Don was an insecure executive and would not take a bullet for the troops. Seeing his actions in person made me a believer. Fortunately the CEO knew Don's weaknesses and my strengths. His response to Don's pass the buck comment was, "Don, you're the marketing leader. You're responsible for the content of this presentation. Don't give me that "Kenny didn't do — crap."

I realized the true leader in the room was the CEO sitting across from me not the so called leader who was my boss.

Years later I was put in a position to step up and be responsible. My President was either bright or lucky. I believe he was and is bright — very bright. The year before the "dot.com" bubble burst, Jose took our company Infonet Services Corporation public and received a lot of cash. Jose promoted me to the Senior Director of Mergers and Acquisitions (M&A) reporting to him. My job was to form a team and invest in early stage companies.

My team consisted of legal and financial people. We were a great team with an enormous respect for each other's strengths. We also liked each other personally. The job was challenging for us because the business plans presented to us were pure "dot.com." Except for a very few, these early stage companies showed us plans that lost money for three to four years and then made unrealistic profits in years five and six. I know a handful of companies like Google, Yahoo, Amazon and eBay had business plans like the ones described and became powerhouses. However, that is just a few out of the tens of thousands of "dot.com" companies that failed. The bust happened because investors realized the insanity of putting up millions in companies that only had an idea and unrealistic business plans.

My team was "old school." We didn't buy into the vast majority of these companies' business plans. We wanted to see real revenue results and a finished product before we would consider investing. Because of this, meeting Jose's objectives was difficult.

One day Jose presented us with a company that was synergistic with our company. Digital Island was a two year old company that had twenty five million dollars in revenue their second year of operation. However, they were still losing money. They approached Jose because they needed money to grow the business and become profitable.

They had a reasonable business plan, but it was predicated on changing their business from a server hosting company to an internet networking company. My team and I believed server hosting was a dying business. We did like the internet networking business because it was growing at an above average rate and was synergistic with our company. We also liked the management team running the company.

Our problem was twofold. First, internet networking was a new business for them. Ninety percent of their current revenue was coming from the hosting business. The second issue was the critical one for the team and me. Digital Island wanted one hundred million dollars for twenty five percent of the company. In our opinion a four hundred million dollar evaluation for a twenty five million dollar company that had not yet returned a profit was not acceptable. Digital Island's management was not being ridiculous. Those were the kind of crazy evaluations given to "dot.com" companies before the bust.

My President was excited about doing this deal. He was going to be on the board of the company. He believed the synergy between the two companies would enable them to meet their long term goals. We liked Digital Island and their plans with our company. We just didn't like the price and the fact that one hundred million dollars would not even get us a controlling interest in the company. We believed Infonet could have spent less money and delivered the same internet service by doing it themselves. Jose didn't agree. He had been right so many times, but this time we felt he was wrong.

My team and I had two choices. Do the deal knowing that would please Jose. Why not, it would be years before we would know if it was a good deal or a bad deal. The other choice was to tell Jose I didn't agree with him and would not sign off on the deal. I choose the latter. I knew there was a chance Jose would disband my team and possibly demote me into another job. My team told me they had my back and would take the hit with me. I told them I was the leader and this decision was on me. I appreciated their support, but knew I had to be accountable.

Digital Island was insisting on a decision. Jose was out of the country in meetings. His administrator told me he would only take emails for the next two days. I sent an email describing the reasons I was not willing to go through with the deal. Three hours later I received a call from him. He was stern in his comments. He reviewed the reasons with me in what I thought was his way of trying to change my mind. That was not his goal. He was trying to determine if I was committed to my decision. He asked if my team agreed with me. I told him this decision was my responsibility.

Much to my surprise Jose accepted my position. He did remind me that it was my decision and if Digital Island met or exceeded the business plans they projected he would hold me accountable. I accepted his response. My team and I rejoiced partly because we believed we were right and partly because we didn't get demoted.

As a side note, Cable and Wireless (C&W) purchased Digital Island a few months later for six hundred million dollars. Months later the "dot.com" bubble burst. Digital Island no longer exists. I assumed it was integrated into C&W and never lived up to its projections.

Taking responsibility and being willing to be accountable are key elements to help you build confidence. Once built, you're on the road toward presence.

Commitment

Leaders are committed. It shows in their words, their eyes and even their body language. The leaders' energy toward their commitment to a task must reflect in the people they lead. It's that energy that creates presence.

A leader can't get things done if the people they lead are just going through the motions. They need people who are as committed as them. However, commitment can't be demanded. It's the leader's responsibility to instill commitment to a project or task.

The best fighting force in the world is one that is committed. It's the leader's job to instill into the troops the reasons they should be willing to risk their lives. It's important to give the troops all the tools they need to win, but tools alone will not win wars. The United States learned that lesson in the Vietnam War.

Business is war. The leaders' people need tools to accomplish their job. More importantly, they need to clearly understand why success is critical to the team, department and the company. They need to know why their commitment to an assignment is critical. They need to know their peers and especially their leader is committed to the task.

Committed leaders have confidence.

Not Being Defensive

Leadership comes with criticism. There is no way to avoid it. A leader will try to get a consensus from everyone, but will go forward if some disagree. The Naysayers are ready to pounce on the leader if the slightest thing goes wrong. "I told you so" is their mantra.

Leaders have to have thick skins. Overreacting to criticism is a sign of insecurity and might be interpreted as self-doubt. If you believe you're right, if you believe the steps you're taking will deliver the projected results, if you believe you will find a new way to make it happen should the current way not go as planned, then you don't have to defend your position to the Naysayers.

Handling criticism may be harder than making the decision. Naysayers think you're wrong even before your plan has had time to work. Naysayers try to create self-doubt by saying, "This will never work." Before you respond to them ask yourself, "If I fight back, will I change their minds? If I do everything in my power to convince them I'm right, will they roll over and say, "I'm sorry, I didn't understand — you're right and I am wrong."

It is rare that people with an entrenched position will change their minds. Many of them stop listening once they have formed a strong opinion. It's not important to change their minds. What is important is to accept their opinion. True leaders listen to the Naysayers opinion. True leaders evaluate their opinion. After evaluation, true leaders either set a new direction or thank the Naysayers for their input, but make it clear they are staying with their original decision.

Defending your position to the death is as wrong as the Naysayers not being willing to be open minded to your approach. If *you* stop listening you will never get *them* to listen. Criticism is good. Criticism is democratic. Listening to criticism is good — avoiding it is not leading. Having the strength to listen to the Naysayers instead of putting them down is a true sign of your presence.

I like to tell this story:

Joe reaches into his pocket and finds a quarter. He puts the quarter in his hand and makes a fist. When a friend approaches he tells her he found a quarter in his pocket and now has it in his hand. His friend says to him, "You don't have a quarter in your hand. As a matter of fact you don't have *any* money." Joe insists he has the quarter in his hand. She insists he doesn't. The more he insists the more the friend resists.

After a lot of back and forth Joe starts to think, "Maybe I don't have the quarter in my hand anymore. Maybe I dropped it without knowing. Maybe it was never a quarter in the first place."

Obviously Joe was lacking in confidence. If Joe was a confident person he would not feel the need to defend the quarter in his hand to his friend. He would know he had the quarter and would not doubt if it was still in his hand.

A confident Joe would have said to his friend, "Listen, I know you don't believe I have a quarter in my hand, but that's *your* problem. I know I have this quarter, so let's go buy a pack of gum."

Think about this story in your every day business and personal life. How many fights do you have with your spouse, friends, family, co-workers and upper management that could be avoided if you didn't feel the need to defend yourself?

Leaders don't have the luxury of being defensive. Blaming the outside world for decisions that go wrong will eliminate you from the leadership role. No one wants to hear "It's not me it's them." No one will look up to a person whose reason for failure is a list of actions others could or should have taken that would have changed the outcome. A true leader will always start a sentence with an "I" or at least a "We." He will never start that sentence with a "They."

A leader's response to failure should contain 10% reasons why and 90% solutions on how they will improve the situation, resolve the problem and what they will do to avoid the failure in the future.

Presence will never be gained by being defensive. Presence will happen when you're viewed as a confident leader who is willing to admit a mistake and is focused on the solution of the problem instead of who caused the problem.

Not being defensive means you have confidence. Confident leaders project presence.

Figure Out How You Can — Not Why You Can't

People always look up to others that get things done. People look up to someone who never acts defeated. Confident leaders see a barrier as something to jump over. The leader's attitude is, "It's never too high." Their response is, "How high do I have to jump." A leader will get people to do things they never thought they could do. When others are defeated the leader will encourage and push them to figure out how to accomplish the task.

Many people give up too soon. If a batter looks at the top baseball pitcher in the league and thinks they don't have a chance of getting a base hit, guess what, they will not get a hit. Confident people always believe today is my day. Even if they never had a base hit off of this pitcher before, they will still believe this is the time it will happen. A true leader will plan a strategy on how to get a hit. Maybe the best approach is to bunt instead of swinging at the pitch.

A confident leader will never make it easy for someone to say no to him or her. Not achieving is easier than achieving. Saying it can't be done is the easy way out. Figuring out how you can is not as easy, but the reward is worth the effort. The reward is the satisfaction derived from completing the task, the learning gained from figuring out how to do it, the respect received from others who didn't think it could be done and the knowledge that, "I've done it once — I can do it again." Confident leaders will encourage their people by saying, "I believe it can be done. If you really try to think of a solution you will solve the problem."

There may be a price to pay for this "can do" attitude. The only solution available to a problem may be unpleasant. It could require a sacrifice. It may be risky. It may require a major change in your life.

One reason we struggle to find solutions to problems is because we don't want to consider answers that are unpleasant. To name just a few:

- Who is willing to propose a solution that might cost them their job — a confident leader!

- Who is willing to propose a solution that may result in him or her losing some of their income — a confident leader!

- Who is willing to propose a solution that may lead to a friend, a son, a daughter or wife dropping you from their life — a confident person!

Confident people make shit happen. They take action. They aren't frozen by inaction. Confident people don't accept no as an answer to tough problems — they push for another solution. Confident people don't try to make political decisions. Confident people don't try to make popular decisions. Confident people aren't concerned about how they are perceived. They are confident that the perception of others will be positive.

Leaders with confidence have presence and are true leaders.

BUILDING BLOCK FOUR
COMMUNICATION

Communication is achieved through

- *Knowledge*
- *Strategic Thinking*
- *Confidence*
- Good Listener
- Credibility
- Resolve/Commitment
- Salesmanship

Knowledge, Strategic Thinking and Confidence

Communication is the next building block on the path toward presence. Having *knowledge* is important when communicating. The more you know about the subject the easier it's to communicate your point. The more information you have about the world around you the easier it will be to answer questions from others. The more knowledge you have the more interesting you will be as a communicator.

As a *strategic thinker* you will be perceived as a communicator with a vision. People listen intently when the person speaking is discussing their vision of the future. People are attracted to leaders who can discuss their vision of the future as well as their knowledge of the past and the present.

Confidence is critical to communicating. You're much more credible when you communicate with confidence. People will listen better when you speak with confidence. If you don't have confidence, you don't have a prayer of getting up in front of an audience and speaking. This is especially true if you're about to speak to your peers instead strangers. If you try to do so the audience will sense your fear and insecurity. Without confidence you will be uncomfortable and not having fun. Without confidence, speaking to an audience will feel like a punishment instead of an opportunity.

If you have knowledge, strategic thinking, confidence and communication, presence is within your reach.

Good Listener

The first step to becoming a good communicator is to become a good listener. Your audience is made up of good and bad listeners. You have to understand both. You have to be empathic to the ones who aren't good listeners. You need to understand why they have trouble listening.

You might wonder, "Why is their listening problem my problem?" The answer is because the burden of communicating is on you. You have to accept that responsibility. If you don't, you will talk a lot without communicating very much. "What counts is in the mind of the listener."

What you have to say is meaningless if the people to whom you're speaking aren't listening. The information you're trying to communicate is worthless if the mind of the listener hears something different. Therefore, testing for understand is your burden not theirs.

Listening is a learned skill. Some children are quiet when someone is speaking. However, that doesn't mean they are listening. When they get older they act the same way. They are quiet, but are they listening. Some children continue to talk over people that are speaking to them. When they get older they continue the same behavior. Many of us fall in one of those two categories. I'm in the talking over people category. Which are you?

Listening was very hard for me. I'm bright. I believed I could perceive what the speaker was trying to tell me before all the words came out of his mouth. My way was to only hear the beginning of what they had to say, interrupt them and proceed to tell them what they were trying to communicate. I failed more times than I succeeded. It frustrated them because they felt I was not listening. While I thought I was speeding things up, in reality, I was slowing things down.

To be a good listener you have to open your mind to listening. Remove your prejudices of the person who is speaking. Nobody wants to admit it, but many of us have a problem listening to a fat person, a short person, a person who speaks with a ghetto tongue, an extremely beautiful woman, a real ugly or disfigured man or woman, or worst yet, your parents or your children.

It took me a long time to realize that someone not knowledgeable on a subject many times says the smartest things. I realize now that most of us see situations differently from others. Even the slightest difference in perspective could create a huge change in my view of the situation.

One of the most important ways I can broaden my world is by listening to others. I can enhance my presence by being a good listener. Even if I only get one small idea or change of perspective, it's worth listening. I have changed many decisions based upon inputs from people whom I didn't think knew the subject or were too verbose trying to get their point across. Had I shut them out I would have made the wrong decision.

If you don't listen to the people you lead they will think you don't respect what they have to say. They will not believe their input matters. "Why should I follow someone who never hears me?" "Why should I follow someone who, when I speak, it goes in one of his ears and out the other?" "Why should I try to have original thoughts when my leader is not interested to hear them?"

Yes, there are many leaders who want followers to only do what they are told. These leaders put themselves above everyone else. Their way is the only way. These so called leaders believe that allowing their followers to have input or an opinion on a subject will open the door to rebellion. These aren't true leaders.

Don't confuse listening with decision making. Even in the military, true leaders listen to their troops. They don't have to take action on what they suggest. However, they do listen. If one of their troops tells them they believe the enemy might be on the other side of the hill, the true leader will check it out. Only a poor leader would not listen and forge ahead because they didn't respect any input from the people they lead.

Listening requires the patience and the desire to listen. You have to believe that effective listening will enhance your life, your teams' life and make you a better leader with more presence.

Your DNA and your upbringing may have made you into an outgoing gregarious people loving person. Unfortunately those traits don't guarantee you will be a good communicator or a good listener. To be a good communicator you have to want to communicate what you know and what you want from others. The following is the minimum you have to do to be an effective listener:

- Think about what you want to say before you say it. This will enable you to formulate your statements in a way others can understand and *hear* your communication.

- It would be very helpful if you wrote down what you want to communicate and read it back to yourself to see if *you* can get the message. If *you* can't get the message others won't either.

- An effective communicator has to be sensitive to the emotional state of the people with whom they are trying to communicate. If you deliver your message in a way that others can't or don't want to hear, you have failed as an effective communicator. Let me give you an example:

  You want to ask an over-worked under paid stressed out skilled hourly employee to work late on an important job. You say, "John, can you work late tonight. It's important."

  You have clearly stated what you want of John. There is no doubt John understood you. However, did he hear you? Even if John needs the extra money it may not be enough to get him to work the extra hours. Even if he works the extra hours, will he do so in a way that will get the job done on time with quality? There needs to be something in it for John other than money.

  What if you said, "John, I know you've been working hard and I appreciate your effort? Our department has an opportunity. We have this important job to get out and if we do it on time senior management will recognize us. I'm not promising it will lead to higher pay or less stress, but it puts us in a better position. It's very important we get this job done tonight. Can you work late?"

  You added sixty two additional words to your request. It took you five seconds longer to say it in a way John can hear you. Those five seconds probably increased your chances of getting John to agree by 90%.

  By acknowledging John's hard work, making him feel part of something and by using words like "we" and "our," the relationship between John and you will improve significantly. This will give you a better chance that John will get the job done with quality that night and help when you need something else from him in the future.

You could have also said, "John, we have this important job that has to get done tonight. Cancel your plans because I need you to work late."

The inference with this statement is, "If you don't work tonight you will either be fired or at a minimum be on my shit list." As a leader this will work — John will stay late. But if a leader needs threats to accomplish the task, he or she is not a true leader of human beings.

Life is too short. Threats just add more stress to your life and the people you threaten. Add the sixty two words. Take the extra five seconds. You will be happier. Your employees will be happier. Life will be better for all.

Think about taking this same approach in your personal life. People don't just lead in business. A spouse can be a leader. A friend can be a leader. Leadership can be rewarding if you communicate in a way that is nonthreatening. Your presence comes out when you communicate this way.

- Pay attention to the listener's body language. Look directly into their eyes. The body and especially the eyes will tell you if they are hearing you. Be sensitive if their eyes say, "I don't understand." If you sense they didn't get it, try saying it another way. Don't wait for them to tell you they didn't get it. They may be embarrassed or don't want to be perceived as someone who is stupid.

  Don't take the attitude, "What, is he an idiot? I couldn't have said it any clearer." As a leader your task is to be an effective communicator. Blaming them for their failure to understand is not leading and not communicating.

Listening is about hearing. The words don't just have to come into your ears and fill your brain. The words have to be heard in a way that your brain is willing to process them. In that process your brain has to make sense of the information and compare it with what you already know or perceive to know. During that process your brain will either build on something you know or create a new original idea.

Effective communications is a critical part of creating a presence. Think about the great leaders you have ever known. It doesn't matter if they are the president of a country, the head of your department or even your best friend. When those people enter a room they may or may not seem to have a presence. However, after communicating with them it will be clear to you that this person has a definite presence.

Credibility

People will listen better if they believe you're credible. Credibility comes from your experiences, knowledge, accomplishments, decision making skills, risk taking skills and display of confidence. The first thought in peoples' mind is, "Why should I listen to this person?"

Be very careful about your facts. If the listener catches one fact wrong they start to believe all the facts are wrong. Don't make bold statements unless you have done the research and checked it twice. Don't make statements of truth from sources of hearsay. Don't make quotes without acknowledging the source. A quote without a statement of source will be perceived as an original quote from you. If you get called on it later your credibility will go down the drain. If you don't know the source make sure the listener knows it's not an original quote.

Credibility is hard to come by. When you're credible on one thing it builds on the next. After much building, you're deemed credible. However, one small chink in your credibility armor could cost you. Once credibility is lost, it will take a long time to get it back.

If you're an astronaut speaking about the International Space Station, the audience will assume you're credible. What if you're not well known — like me?

I was doing lectures on "Taking Charge of Your Career and Your Life" to business venues. When I tried to get UCLA University to let me lecture in their lecture hall, the first question they asked me was, "Are you published?" I was not. The realization of being unknown and not having known credibility, even though I had many years of senior management experience, incented me to write my first book.

After success with my book and many radio and TV appearances, UCLA announced my lecture: "Taking Charge of Your Career and Your Life, by Kenny Felderstein, author of ….. Now that I was a published author I had credibility with the UCLA staff and their students. My senior status at major corporations gave me credibility at business forums, but the book enabled me to expand to cruise ship lectures, TV appearances, radio and others venues.

If you're going to speak to a person or a group of people that don't know you and your accomplishments, send them your resume in advance before telling them up-front why they should perceive you as credible. For example, being on the marketing team that launched the first laser printer, has given me credibility on speaking on a wide range of marketing subjects.

Don't be bashful. "If you have it — flaunt it." Your experiences, knowledge, accomplishments, decision making skills, risk taking skills and display of confidence make you credible. When you're credible, they listen. When they listen, you're communicating. When you're communicating you gain presence.

Resolve/Commitment

Resolve equals commitment to your beliefs and taking action on those beliefs. Resolve within yourself is part of your presence. Backing up your resolve with action increases your presence. Letting them know who you are and what you stand for is part of your resolve and your presence. Telling people the truth even when they don't want to listen to the truth is part of your resolve.

Commitment and resolve to the information you're communicating will help get people to listen. Resolve and commitment shows up in your body language. It's heard through your voice. Sometimes pounding the table is a good thing. It shows how much resolve you really have. Using controlled anger as opposed to uncontrollable anger to make a point is a communication technique.

People have told me that I'm intense when I speak. I take that input as a compliment. When I communicate to an individual or a group I *am* intense. I truly believe in the information I'm communicating. I'm showing my resolve and commitment with my words, my voice and my body.

Having resolve is usually considered a positive thing. Being intense is sometimes considered a negative thing. I choose not to see a difference. I like communicators who are intense. I'm not threatened by their intensity as long as they aren't over the top, have credibility and care about me as a listener. I view their intensity as resolve and commitment. Having that attribute makes me want to listen, makes them interesting and makes me see the presence within them.

Resolve and committed people live by the "now" philosophy. However, most people live by the "tomorrow" philosophy. Timing is everything. In business putting something off one day could lose you a sale. I've had it happen to me.

Many years ago when I was a Xerox sales manager, one of my sales guys waited until our Friday weekly meeting to surprise my team and me with good news. The head of the LA Times data center wanted us to come in and sign a big order for our newest laser printers. In today's dollars it amounted to over three million. Immediately after our meeting I instructed Larry to call the customer and make an appointment to sign that day. He had trouble getting through all morning and finally, after lunch, was able to reach the executive's administrator.

Sometime after 2pm Larry came in to see me. His face told a story I was not going to like. "Kenny, the contract signing is not going to happen today." "Is it because he's not in the office" I said? "Worse," he frowned. "The administrator told me he had a heart attack last night and is in the hospital." "Is he going to be OK," I said half concerned about the customer and half concerned about the status of our three million dollar deal. "I couldn't get any more information. They told me to call back Monday."

That Saturday the customer died. It was a sad day for him and his family and a bad day for my branch office.

A week and a half later my sales rep and I were sitting in front of the new head of the Los Angeles Times data center. He was a very pleasant man with many years of management experience at the Times. His prior executive job was in the Times financing department. Larry had only met him once which was one more than I. We both should have had a closer relationship with all the senior executives at the Times.

I didn't have to hear the words coming out of his mouth because his body language told the story. In a caring and uncomfortable way he said, "Guys, I know you worked hard to place your equipment in the Time's data center. I was told your system and your service is excellent. Larry has won many friends here at the Times."

Waiting for the "but" that stabs you right in the heart is something you never get used to. He continued, "But, I'm new in this job. I'm not a data center professional. I was brought in here because of my finance knowledge and my relationship with senior management." He kept speaking without taking a pause, "Senior management has never heard of your expertise in data processing. Their only experience is their administrator's use of your Xerox copiers. When they think of data processing they think IBM. Since almost all of the other equipment in the data center is from IBM, I'm sorry to tell you that I'm going to play it safe and go with IBM's laser printers."

Larry gave it a valid try, but we both knew we had lost. The new guy was not a risk taker. He was going to do what was politically acceptable to management. At least he was up front about it.

Larry was told the previous Tuesday he won the order. He could have wrapped up all the paperwork that day. The data center manager didn't get ill until late Thursday night. There was plenty of time to close the deal. The only reason he waited until Friday was because he didn't feel a sense of urgency and wanted to look good in front of me and the other sales people at our Friday sales meeting. In sales, time is never on your side. Also in sales "NOW" is the only answer.

How many of you put off until tomorrow what you know you can do today? Many times it's not because of laziness. Most of the time it's because you don't have the resolve and commitment that creates the necessary urgency. The consequences of waiting aren't known. Doing it "now" means confronting the situation "now." Since you don't have knowledge that something bad will happen if you wait, some people will put off the possibility of confrontation until later.

A leader has to make sure the people he leads have a sense of urgency. He can't be around them all the time. Therefore, he has to impress upon them it's in their and the team's best interest not to procrastinate. He can try to condition them with the carrot, but has to be willing to use the stick if they show a tendency to putting things off.

A true leader with presence has resolve and commitment to the "NOW." His followers must attack life "now." Now is the time to close that sale. Now is the time to read that book you always wanted to read. Now is the time to seek the help to improve your life. Now is the time to put that business case together. Now is the time to get married or divorced. Now is the time to ask for a raise. Now is the time to have that meeting with senior management. Now is the time to try to break the record you believe you can achieve. Now is the time to get the presence necessary to lead.

Salesmanship

Many people see salesmanship as sleazy. I will agree there are some sleazy salesmen or saleswomen. I was a professional salesman and hold that trade with high regard. My definition of salesmanship is, "Convincing the customer that what he wants to buy is what I have to offer." Great salesmen can handle objections at the moment they are offered. Exceptional sales people are great communicators. Excellent communicators are able to convince the individual or the audience that what they are saying is what they want to hear. Outstanding salespeople have all the building blocks of presence. Add a little DNA and they display a great presence.

I have worked hard to be a better communicator. I stunk at it in my early years. I was a bad listener. I didn't think I needed credibility. My position was that if they don't think I'm credible that's their problem. I thought they should listen because I spoke well, was animated and had a great deal of resolve. I was insisting they listen to me. I never tested for understanding because I thought that was their responsibility.

My years in sales and sales leadership humbled me and taught me a lot about communicating. Fortunately, I was a willing learner. I took communication classes. I watched great sales people communicate. I was willing to see my defects and make the changes necessary. I now consider myself a good communicator.

One characteristic a true leader must have is the ability to sell their ideas to everyone. Think about the leaders of the world and their ability to sell. I really hate to admit this, but even Hitler was a great communicator. He took a country that was in big financial trouble and got the working class, the elite and the military to believe that his strategy was the way to make Germany financially sound and powerful.

People needed jobs so he built a huge military. People needed a scapegoat for their problems and the country's problems. Hitler got most of the people to believe it was the Jews and anyone else who were not of German origin. The solution was to eliminate them off the face of the earth. Don't believe it was just a few crazies who followed Hitler in this extinction. It was common people who were so down on their luck they were willing to listen to and believe a strong salesman who told them that killing Jews and others would make their lives better.

In the end what I stated in the forward won out and the bully fell from his leadership post.

Please don't think that I applaud Hitler or the others in this world today that are using peoples' race, color or religious beliefs as scapegoats to lead their countries, communities, or groups. This is the negative way of leadership and in the end they will fail. However, you can't say they aren't leaders with excellent communication skills. Sadly, the world is full of people that will follow the devil straight to hell.

Are these negative leaders' true leaders — NO! We all know who were and are the true leaders with presence. They are the leaders that lead for the good of mankind. A true leader of a country cares about all the people he or she leads and works hard to make their lives better. A true leader communicates to all of the people his strategy to improve their lives. A true national leader cares about the other countries around the world and wishes their people happiness.

Some believe the heavy emphasis on media is not fair because the national leader, when communicating, has to look good and sound good in this electronic world. I strongly don't agree with that point of view. Today's multimedia opens the door to hundreds of millions more people than before. This gives national voters, other world leaders and the global population a chance to see and hear how the leader will lead.

What it does mean is that the leaders of today must have presence. It's their presence that will come across on the TV and the Web. It's their presence that will enable them to communicate so that everyone will listen. If a leader doesn't have presence and is a poor salesperson she or he will have a very hard time winning over the people they are trying to lead.

My focus above is on local, national and world leaders. Does that mean corporate, community and group leaders don't need presence and don't have to be excellent communicators? Absolutely not! Just because these leaders aren't on TV doesn't mean they don't have to be excellent salesmen with a strong presence. Today, most corporate, community and group interaction is done via room video conferencing, web video conferencing and audio conferencing. Even in one on one and one on many communications presence is critical in getting their position heard and acted on by the people receiving the message.

Almost every company, community and group has a perceived hierarchy where one is supposed to be more important the higher up you go. I don't see it that way. The maintenance people in a company have a job that if not done will make the people that benefit from their services less effective. Think about executives having to clean their desk and take out the trash every night. Therefore, maintenance people, if professional, have an important role in the company, community and group. Treating them as professionals and communicating effectively to them will increase everyone's productivity.

Presence and effective communication to everyone, regardless of their rank, is not only required to be a true leader it's just sound business acumen. Everyone wants to know how the company, community and the group are performing. Many times leaders think that people in lower paid jobs don't care to know. That is an urban legend. True leaders who communicate to everyone at all levels and make them feel part of the big picture will be more respected than leaders who don't appreciate the efforts of the "little people."

BUILDING BLOCK FIVE
PERSONAL PRESENTATION

Personal Presentation is achieved through

- *Knowledge*

- *Strategic Thinking*

- *Confidence*

- *Communication*

- Physical Body Language and Voice Fluctuation

- Dress for Success

- Facial Features and Gestures

Knowledge, Strategic Thinking, Confidence and Communication

Personal presentation is the fifth building block on the stairway to presence. Personal presentation is about how you look, how you carry yourself and your physical presence. I like to think of personal presentation as the outer shell or protective covering over the other building blocks of presence. Packaging *knowledge, strategic thinking, confidence* and *communication* inside the well made box of personal presentation will give you presence. Adding a little DNA will take you from very good presence to outstanding presence.

By the way, very good presence is what most leaders strive for. I believe I have very good presence. Only a slim few have outstanding presence. When you see and sense outstanding presence you will know the difference.

Physical Body Language and Voice Fluctuation

Your body can show how serious you are about a subject or task. Your body can show happiness or sadness. Your body can show anger and disappointment. Your body can show your resolve and commitment. Your body can show confidence. Make sure you use your body to show your presence.

Body language plays a role in communication. Someone standing behind a podium reading off their notes is boring. Boring makes you stop listening. Boring is the antithesis of presence. When communicating to a group it helps to be animated.

Personally, I don't like podium speaking. I like to move around when I speak. Some say doing so is distracting. I believe a moving target makes you concentrate on the speaker more than a still image. I believe movement is more interesting than stagnation. I don't just run around the stage. Many times I use movement to make a point.

For example, when discussing fear of failure, I show that some people think that if they make a decision or take a risk that doesn't work, management will be mad at them. Then their fearful brain tells them they might get fired. Their fearful brain then says, "If I get fired I won't have any money. If I don't have any money, my spouse will leave me and my friends and family will abandon me. With no money and no loved ones I might wind up on the streets. If I'm on the streets I'll probably die."

I show this fearful brain's progression by starting at one end of the stage while moving over to the other end at each progression. Then I say to the audience, "Fear of failure can get the brain to go from a potential bad decision to death." While I'm saying this I move from the place I'm standing to the other end of the stage. I then go back to the middle of the stage and explain how ridiculous the fearful brain is when it knows that even if the worst happens we will always have food to eat, air to breath and shelter.

After doing this lecture many times and seeing the audiences' reaction, I know this expression of fear via movement is very effective.

If you must speak from behind a podium voice fluctuation is critical. Emphasizing key points must be done via the fluctuation of your voice. If you choose to move around, voice fluctuation is still critical in getting your key points across. In the example above I always use voice fluctuation in addition to my movement to get the audience from a poor decision to death.

The information below is about physical body language you can do something about. Poor physical conditions out of your control have their disadvantages, but should not prevent others from sensing your presence.

Men or women over six feet tall are perceived to have presence when they enter a room. Once people get over their height their advantage vanishes unless they really have presence. Average height people are just that — average. They have no advantage from a presence point of view. Little people (under five feet) have a presence advantage. They, like the very tall stand out in the crowd. Again, their advantage will diminish quickly unless they truly have presence.

If you don't have a physical body presence advantage you need to consider how you treat your body. Good health is not only important to your life it's important to your presence. Sickly people don't have good presence. I am not speaking about people with a serious disease or a physical handicap.

My wife's Uncle Bernie had multiple sclerosis and spent a large part of his life in a wheelchair. The first time I met Bernie, I could immediately sense his presence. It was clear to me Bernie had presence just by watching how others acted around him. Another example is Christopher Reeve who after his accident showed his great presence.

Good posture is not only good for your health it's important to your presence. If you're not born with good posture you have to work on it. Ellen has to always remind me about my posture. I have to think about it when I communicate to others — especially to a large audience.

Weight control is important to presence. You don't have to be a body builder. You don't have to be thin. A little pot in your belly is OK. A large pot in your belly is not OK. If you have a bad body shape people will think, "If he or she can't take care of their body why should I listen to them." Having people focused on your poorly shaped body will make it tougher for them to let your presence through.

Dress For Success

How you dress will have an impact on the way you are perceived. Leaders who are sloppy dressers will be looked upon by others as people who don't take the time to care about themselves. They will think, "If they don't care about themselves, why should I respect them as my leader?" If a sloppy dresser enters a room, people will be focused on his dress not on his presence.

You can dress casual if you're not sloppy and you're leading the right audience for that style. Over dressing is almost as bad as sloppy dressing. For example, if you're going to lead a team of software programmers in a two thousand dollar suit and tie they will not think of you as one of them. Software programmers believe they are more productive when dressed casually. I was one of them and I agree. On the other hand, a suit and tie is a prerequisite when dealing with bankers.

You don't have to over dress so they will be reminded that you're different — you are their leader. Your leadership skills and your presence will dictate your leadership role. When JFK was asked why he didn't wear expensive designer suits he said, "When you *are* the president you don't have to look like you are the president."

Xerox was a suit and tie company. Since I came from the computer company Xerox purchased, I would show my non-conformity by wearing plaid shirts (instead of white or blue shirts) and many times I didn't wear a tie. I hated ties then and still do today.

George Bryan "Beau" Brummell created the "British Look" in the early 19th century. This was the first suit and tie. To this day I have no idea why that "uniform" has lasted so long. It's expensive and a buttoned-up shirt with a knotted tie is very uncomfortable. Uncomfortable is not a productive way to work.

I was the first in my division to create casual Fridays. The executives thought we came into work while we were on vacation. When they realized we were dressing that way every Friday they were not happy. However, the Xerox employee handbook didn't mandate a suit and tie. It only stated that you had to be dressed in a neat and appropriate manner. The main reason the executives didn't stop us was because my team was one of the most productive in our division. Xerox today, like many companies, is business casual every day.

When I decided to leave Xerox I interviewed with Symantec's Peter Norton Group on a Tuesday. This is the group that created the virus protection on most of our computers. Coming from Xerox, I showed up at Symantec in a white shirt and a sport jacket. While sitting in the waiting room I noticed the software engineers, administrators, managers and others passing me were dressed casually. I am not talking about business casually; I'm talking about tee shirts and jeans. The software engineers stared at me with eyes that said, "This guy might be a narcotics agent."

I interviewed with the president of the Peter Norton Group who was dressed like the software engineers. When we were done he said he wanted me to come back on Friday to meet other managers. I left him and went to his administrator to set a time for that coming Friday. After doing so she said to me, "Kenny, Friday is casual day around here." I was shocked. Did that mean cut off shorts and tank tops? I joined the company and have not worn a suit for business since.

The bottom line, wear clothes that fit your body, fit in with your company or group, make you feel confident and are not distracting. You want them to focus on your presence not what you're wearing.

Facial Features and Gestures

"Your eyes are the pathway to your presence." Let me say it another way, "Your presence will show in your eyes." Your facial features and gestures will speak without words. Great actors can tell an entire story without uttering a word. Make sure your facial features and gestures are communicating what you want others to see — not always what you feel.

You can't just look good you have to be a good actor. Good acting goes a long way in looking like a leader. A good actor is believable because his body language and his facial features and gestures relates to the words that come out of his mouth.

If you're down in the dumps because of problems at work or in your personal life you don't have the luxury to display that emotion to the people you lead. They need to see you as a positive person. Even though you're having an awful day your facial features and gestures must show a positive facade.

You should decide if you want your facial features or your words to communicate your disappointment with an individual or your team. It's possible to say nothing and just let them see you're upset by the way you manipulate your body and face. It's also possible to have a stoic face and let your words do the talking.

In my opinion, facial gestures have a bigger impact on people than words. Facial gestures are defined by the person who sees them. If they know they screwed up, they will interpret your facial features in the worst possible way. Your words can be less threatening and more supportive while you're telling them what they did wrong. You can also do both. As a leader, it's your choice. Make sure you choose the one that will be the most productive and will prevent the problem from happening again.

Presence is something others feel. Personal presentation is what others see. It's the well made wrapper around the other building blocks of presence.

BUILDING BLOCK SIX
LEADERSHIP TRAITS

Leadership Traits **are achieved through:**

- *Knowledge*

- *Strategic Thinking*

- *Confidence*

- *Communication*

- *Personal Presentation*

- Trust

- Passion

- Leads by Example

- Customer Focused

- Process Improvement Oriented

- Politically Balanced

- Bottom Line Oriented

- Goal Oriented

- Rewards Accomplishment

- Market Driven

- Creates a Workable Culture and a Productive and Fun Environment

- Doesn't Hide Behind the Process

- Accountability

- Promotes Teamwork

- Empowers Employees

- Makes it Easy to be Replaced

You will not become a true leader with presence if you only have mastered the first five building blocks. To reach that goal you need to have excellent leadership traits. The traits stated below are what I consider the most important.

Trust

Trust is something that can be lost in a minute and take years to regain. A person will be totally ineffective as a leader if the people he wants to lead don't trust him.

Never lie — even by omission. Never tell someone to do something without explaining to them the known consequences. Never put a person in a position to fail when you strongly believe they will do so. Never take credit for something another has done. Being self-serving will destroy trust.

As a leader, I have always given my trust to the people I deal with day to day. Distrusting people before getting to know them is not leading. You have to be strong and secure enough to trust people without proof. On the other hand, if a person does something to lose your trust you should be very cautious before trusting them again.

Don't assume trust or distrust based upon what someone else says. Make your own decision. It's OK to have a "flag" in the back of your mind about a person based upon what others have said, but you're the leader — you're the decision maker.

Many times in my career I have been told by others, "Watch out for that guy" or "That person is not reliable" or "Don't trust her — she will stab you in the back." Most of the time the person in question was nothing like the description I was getting. By listening to them, respecting them or managing them differently, most turned out to be good employees.

Passion

The leadership characteristic I personally like the most is passion. I love people that are passionate about life. I am attracted to and want to be the kind of person that loves life, loves what they do in life and loves to lead. Passionate people don't lead because of the money, ego or power. They lead because they love living it and doing it.

Passion shows in the person's body language. Enthusiasm shows in the person's eyes. Fervor shows in the person's speech. When you're with a passionate person you become passionate. It's like seeing a beautiful sunset over the ocean. Once you experience it you want to see it every day. Passion begets passion.

A very good friend of mine lived life with great passion. Hal died too early, but got more out of life than most people who live a long time. One of the statements I made at his service was, "Being with Hal was like the wind blowing through my hair."

If you're a person with all the leadership traits discussed in this Building Block and have a passion for what you're doing and life in general, you're the person I personally will follow to the end of the rainbow.

Leads by Example

Leading by example is often confused with doing the job yourself. A poor leader believes in the statement, "If you want something done right do it yourself." It's hard to delegate when you have the capability to accomplish the task yourself. If you don't have the capability to accomplish the task it's easier to lead others to perform because you don't have a choice.

Leadership by example means that the people you lead know you will hold up your end of the bargain. They have to *see* you work hard, take calculated risks, make commitments, fulfill your commitments, make decisions, fight for them, respect them, root for them and achieve the final result. If the people know you will do all you can to succeed they will follow your lead.

They don't have to see you as the person who can do their job better. They don't have to view you as the expert who knows their job better. They don't have to see you jump in and save the day by accomplishing what they could not. You're their leader not their super peer. You have your job (leader/manager) and they have their job. Let them see how well you do your job. Let them see how hard you try to improve yourself. The more they see your dedication and performance the more they will want to follow you.

Coach Red Auerbach is a good example. He won nine basketball championships with the Boston Celtics. Red never played professional basketball so he couldn't do — he had to lead. Red's team pushed themselves beyond their normal capabilities because they believed Red did also. Red was not liked by many in his sport because he worked so hard, pushed himself and others (including Celtic management) to get what he wanted for his team. He also made strategic decisions on and off the court that were not popular, but right.

Talent wise the Boston Celtics were not always the best team in the league. However, they were the most motivated team because a true leader, with presence, led them by example.

Customer Focused

Leaders understand that at any point in time they are either a customer or a supplier. It's easy to relate to the external customer. That is the person or entity using or could be using the products or services you're offering. In business you sell a product to a "customer." The way you should treat your customer is clear. The statement "The customer is always right" is an accepted phrase.

As the supplier to your customer you have certain responsibilities. You have to tell the truth. You have to deliver what you sold. You have to make commitments. You have to meet your commitments. You have to take ownership of all responsibilities even if the people or the companies who support you don't deliver. It is unacceptable to tell your customer, "It's not my fault — *they* didn't deliver." Your customer sees you as his supplier. You're on the front line and have to assume the buck stops with you.

It's not as easy to relate to your internal customers. Yes, leaders and followers have internal customers. A sales representative is counting on product marketing to deliver the product with pricing and proper marketing materials so she can sell to her customer. A soldier is expecting the people at home to deliver to him a gun with bullets so he can defend himself against his enemy. In these cases product marketing and the military distribution platoon are the *suppliers.*

Let's go one level deeper. Product marketing is expecting product development, manufacturing and finance to deliver the product and the pricing information they need so they can deliver to their customer — the sales representative. The military distribution platoon is expecting the manufacturer to deliver the guns and ammo required for their customer — the soldier.

I assume you have guessed by now that product marketing and the military distribution platoon expect to be treated like customers by *their* suppliers.

In my years of management experience I have discovered that almost everyone in a company treats the entity that buys the product and brings in the revenue as a customer. I have also discovered that many people in a company or group don't treat their internal customers the same way. A true leader understands that his department, company or group has to treat both external and internal customers with the same respect. When they are in the customer role they should expect and demand to be treated like a customer. When they are in the supplier role they have to act as a responsible supplier to their internal customer.

There are no compromises in quality leadership. If every leader in the chain performs as a quality leader by understanding and accepting their groups' customer/supplier roles, the end user (external customer) of your product or service will continue to be everyone's valued customer.

I learned these customer/supplier roles and responsibilities in a one week Xerox training class given to senior managers. Some of us agreed with the concepts we were taught and followed them throughout our business and personal life. Others were really into it during the class, but when it was over they went back to their old ways.

Jerry, the VP of manufacturing, and I were on the same team during the training class. We beat all the other teams and won the first place award. Jerry was a gung-ho participant.

One month after the class I had an issue with the timeframe manufacturing was giving my product marketing team on a new product we were about to launch. I went to see Jerry. "Hi Jerry, my team is telling me they are getting a delivery date on our new product two months later then we agreed upon three weeks ago."

Jerry began giving me a long list of excuses as to why manufacturing couldn't deliver on the original date. Using the customer/supplier skills I learned in class I said to Jerry, "I'm sympathetic to your problems, but as your customer and you as my supplier I need manufacturing to deliver on the promised date so we can launch the product to *our* end user customers on time."

Jerry's response was classical, "Kenny, don't give me that customer supplier crap." I guess Jerry didn't get much out of the customer/supplier class after all. By the way, Jerry was never accepted as a true leader with presence by his peers and employees.

Process Improvement Oriented

The old saying, "If it's not broke — don't fix it" is not always the best leadership policy. Leaders should always be challenging their people on ways they might improve the process they are following. A leader should assume their competition is getting better every day. A true leader wants to improve in every way possible for the good of the company and society.

Change for just the sake of change is not good policy. A leader has to be careful not to make his people feel that if they don't change the process they will be thought of as a non-doer. On the other side of the coin in this finely tuned balancing act, the leader has to make sure his people aren't avoiding the process change because the current process makes them comfortable or they don't want to risk change that might make things worse.

Putting a high reward on changing the process might lead to minimal or negative improvement. Putting a high reward on measurable improvement will work, but has potential drawbacks. If the leader's objective is to enhance the team's dynamics, he or she has to be sensitive that each direct report has an equal opportunity to obtain the reward for process improvement.

An adverse example would be a department head who is running a finely tuned operation and therefore has little opportunity for process improvement versus the department head that has a poorly run operation and probably has a lot of room for improvement. The latter has the best chance to obtain the high reward being offered where the former probably will feel punished for doing a good job in the first place.

Being a leader is never easy. Sometimes a true leader will have to piss off some of his people. Trying to be fair to all might not get the process improvement results needed for the good of the whole. It might not be fair, but if the best way to motivate the poorly run department is to reward them for measurable process improvement, the strong leader will do it. That means dealing with the angry department head who is running a tight ship by finding another way to reward him and his team.

A leader has to keep his focus on the big picture. Process improvement is good for all. Every day a true leader has to get his followers to look at improving the way they do things. The leader has to take all necessary actions to motivate his minions to find and implement process improvement actions even if there is risk involved.

Politically Balanced

Let me start by giving you my definition of playing politics:

- Telling someone what you think they want to hear even though it's not what you believe.

- Playing one person off of another.

- Taking on tasks because they make *you* look good — not because they will help make the department or company successful.

- Promoting yourself as the person who delivered the results without giving credit to the people that supported the effort.

- Socializing with the people that will help your career — not because you enjoy their company.

- Making sure you have positioned the situation so that you can blame someone else if the result is deemed a failure.

- Never saying "no" to senior management.

- Being a Teflon suit — making sure nothing bad sticks to you.

It's hard to separate politics from leadership, but I'm going to try.

"Both have to be both"

Any leader who deals with the general public has to show some political skill. Any leader who has to deal with the desire to get reelected has to kiss a few babies. Any leader who has to work with local, national and foreign governments has to be sensitive to those governments' political wants and needs.

When confined within the walls of the corporation or group, a true leader sheds his or her politics. Decision making doesn't require politics. Prudent risk taking doesn't require politics. Strategic planning doesn't require politics. Managing tasks through people doesn't require politics.

If you need politics to lead in business, you're either a weak leader or you work for a company that has a deep seated political culture. If the latter is true, start today to find a new company. If you have employees who try to get by or ahead using politics, get them out of your group. They will either disrupt your team or stab you in the back.

It has been interesting for me to watch Bill Gates and Steven Jobs mature as leaders. When they started out in business they were apolitical. However, over time they realized they had to adapt to the public and political world around them. Within the wall of their corporation they still maintain their aggressive non-political approach. However, they realized that their leadership style was not serving their corporation or its image within the public and governmental arena.

I'm not saying either one of them have become political animals. What I am saying is that they now understand leadership requires a balance of political and non-political presence.

We all know that politicians are political. What most of us don't know is that the best political leaders are the ones who don't use politics to run their in-house office. The books that have been written about our most respected political leaders state that within the walls of their office they lead their staff without politics. These political leaders also hire direct reports that don't meet my definition of "playing politics." They hire people who know how to balance leadership with politics. The best political leaders have the presence required to lead. They were, are or would be great corporate leaders.

Many years ago I worked for a Marketing Vice President who obtained his position via politics not through leadership. This worked at Xerox because the company's culture was pro-political. Below is an example of Don's behavior.

Don's new boss traveled from his Stamford Connecticut office to his Los Angeles office to meet the marketing department. I had done some research on Frosty. He was not the typical Xerox political executive. Frosty was a true leader who was able to balance politics and production. He also had a great presence.

At ten o'clock that morning Don was in Frosty's office for the meet and greet. The office was huge with a large black desk in front of a wraparound corner window. On the other side of the office was a smaller black circular desk with six chairs. The large desk had a single piece of paper on it. The circular desk had nothing on it.

Frosty stood up from his desk and shook Don's hand while giving him a big hello. He then looked down at the single piece of paper and said, "Don, let's get away from this mess and sit over there (pointing to the circular desk)." After the meeting Don rushed down to his office. He was disorganized and his desk was a mess of papers, reports and books scattered everywhere. He frantically cleaned everything off his desk — much of which he put in my office.

Later that day Frosty came to see me at my office. I am not a neat freak, but add Don's big mess to my little mess and you have a desk that fails the "Xerox clean desk" policy. Frosty and I had a professional and enlightening conversation. He knew a great deal about marketing. His years in sales really shined through. Before he left my office he said to me, "Kenny, tell Don he can take his papers and books back to his office." It took me about a minute to close my mouth.

Frosty kept his desk clean because he was anal not because he thought that was the best way to lead. Don cleaned his desk because he thought it would impress Frosty — he was wrong. Don was not a true leader with presence and Frosty knew it within the first five minutes of their conversation. When he saw Don's unnaturally clean office it justified his first impression.

Bottom Line Oriented

My definition of bottom line oriented has nothing to do with making the numbers at all costs. I believe a leader has to get to the heart of the business issues quickly. If she needs to know what time it is, she doesn't have the luxury of knowing how the clock was built.

Once the leader has the bottom line information, decisions can be made and actions can be taken. Also, once the bottom line is known, the leader can determine what additional information is needed to resolve the issue or what the next step should be.

Many non-leaders are uncomfortable unless they know more than everyone else. They spend so much time getting the details they forget to focus on the key elements of the issue.

A practical example would be:

A software programmer goes to his boss and states that he has just found four bugs in the accounting software. The employee is very stressed about it and wants to show the boss how much he knows about software. He begins telling the boss how he found the bug. Before he gets too far in his conversation the boss says, "What's the impact of these bugs?" The programmer continues describing how the accounting software is designed so he can explain the bugs in detail. The boss interrupts him again and says, "I'm not interested in the details just yet. First I want to know what is going to happen or what is not going to happen because of these bugs."

Finally the programmer says, "These bugs will cause the software to stop accepting asset inputs from two of our districts." The boss again asks, "And what impact will that have on our business?" The programmer thinks for a minute and says, "Well, if we don't fix it now next months' balance sheet will be wrong." The boss finally has the bottom line information required to decide what to do next.

"OK John, here is what I now understand. Our accounting software has four bugs that need to get fixed within the next two to three weeks or we will be recording the wrong assets in our next month balance sheet. Is that right?" "That's right boss." "OK, now tell me only what I need to know about these bugs so we together can figure out the best way to get them fixed in the time frame we have."

The leader doesn't have to be the most technical person in the room. The leader does have to know enough to make good decisions. The leader has to judge how much information is critical to lead. If there is time and the capacity to absorb more information, that's good. Knowledge *is* king. However, if the purpose to press for more information is because the so called leader wants to look smart or look good in front of *his* leadership, then that person has failed the leadership course.

If the response from the boss, when the employee tells him about the problem is, "How did these bugs happen," "Who caused these bugs," "Where in the software did these bugs occur," "Describe the details of these bugs to me," then that boss might completely miss the issue at hand. Instead he might spend valuable time finding someone to blame or learning all about how software is developed. By the time he gets the information he needs the monthly balance sheet could come out with missing assets.

The programmer knows all about the accounting software. The programmer is going to fix the bugs or work with others to fix the bugs. The programmer should get the credit for finding the bugs and get the credit if he fixes them. The leader is not going to get to the top of the leadership/presence class if he or she learns all about software bugs. If it's required to get this information to the higher-ups, the leader should take the software programmer with him to the meeting in case the big wigs are lousy leaders and want to know all about software bugs.

Goal Oriented

All good business men and women are goal oriented. The groups they lead want to know the goals. They want to know why they are doing what is being asked of them. They want to be clear on the objective. They want to know if they have succeeded or failed. Leaders have the obligation to make sure the people they lead are clear on the company's goals, the department's goals, the team's goals and the individual's goals.

To accomplish the above, the leader has to find a way to make sure the organizations above him have established clear goals. This sounds easy, but it's not. Many organizations struggle to get their strategy together. Creating clear goals without a clear strategy usually fails.

True leaders many times have to take it upon themselves to work with the organizations above their group to establish *their* strategy and *their* goals. The leader often has to sell other organizations on why having a clear strategy and clear goals is important to their people. Just because an organization is above you doesn't mean they are run by true leaders.

This is where presence is important. The leader has to have presence when working with upper management. If upper management senses your strong presence they will be more willing to listen to you. If they have presence they will be more attracted to you. Presence begets presence. If upper management are poor leaders with little or no presence they might feel threatened by you. This will not enable you to get agreement on a strategy or goal. They will put you and your team in a position to fail.

I found myself in such a position at Symantec. Once it was clear that things were not going to change, I left the company and went to Infonet Corporation. Infonet's CEO and president was a true leader with a strong presence. He had a clear strategy with clear goals. My team and I were successful.

I could make the same points regarding your personal life. A true leader will take the same approach at home or when they are part of any social group. Even friends should have some kind of goals. Organized social groups must have clear goals. Religious groups need clear goals. Everything I'm stating in this book can be applied to both your personal life and your business life. Leading is not about the venue.

Rewards Accomplishment

It's important to reward accomplishment. However, some leaders give too high a reward to people who are just doing their job. Employees get a salary for doing their job. Kids get free room and board for doing their job. Homemakers get to have a happy family for doing their job. By giving an extra reward for just doing their job, the leader never encourages them to accomplish more than they believed they were capable of accomplishing.

Sales people are slightly different. In sales you use compensation as a way of paying for accomplishment. Sales commission plans motivate via money. The more you sell the more money you get. The compensation plan in itself informs the salesperson what they have to do to get the money they want.

The best sales people will do what the compensation plan encourages them to accomplish not what others might want them to achieve. Therefore, if you want a salesperson to sell a specific product, give them more compensation for that product versus another product. If you want that salesperson to focus on customer satisfaction, enhance their greed based on customer satisfaction surveys, retaining account control or increasing revenue at their existing accounts.

An outstanding salesperson is skillful, has an ego and is motivated by money. Selling is a skill that is part DNA, part upbringing, part training, part experience and a whole lot of presence.

Leading a sales team requires all the leadership and training skills in this and other books. However, the best sales people are self motivated. What the leader needs to realize is that many sales people are usually motivated by ego as much as money. True leaders know how to feed their sales people's ego. Giving them awards in front of their peers and upper management goes a long way.

Sometimes the only thing that works is negative reinforcement. Some sales people only respond to their fear of looking bad because they didn't accomplish their quota. Some leaders will use that fear to motivate by having a team meeting where every sales person has to get up in front of the team and announce their performance to date. I don't like negative motivation techniques and try to avoid them as much as possible. However, to be a true leader you have to do what it takes.

It's important for a leader to understand how to use compensation for achievement. Sales people usually view compensation as currency via a commission. Marketing people usually view compensation as currency via a bonus, acknowledgement from their peers and upper management and most of all, getting promoted. Administrative people usually view compensation as a raise in grade level which includes a salary increase and possibly a promotion. Technical people view compensation as recognition of technical accomplishment and a heightened awareness of their accomplishments by their peers.

The bottom line is a true leader is a motivator. The leader's objective is to get things accomplished through people. Their objective is to make the people they lead feel rewarded via greed, ego or whatever turns them on. When people have pushed themselves beyond what others expect of them and what they expect of themselves, they feel great about their accomplishment. Compensation is one way to acknowledge accomplishment and meet the leader's objectives

Marketing Driven

To comprehend what I mean by marketing driven you have to understand how I am defining marketing. In a marketing oriented business, marketing is the orchestrator of the plan — everybody else in the company are the implementers of that plan. Companies use the term marketing very loosely. In fact there are many types of marketing.

Product marketing defines and delivers the companies products to the sales organization. Channel marketing defines the channel requirements to product marketing. They also train and motivate the channels that sell the products. Marketing communications promotes the company and the products to the outside world. In some companies there is a marketing strategy department that develops future channel, communication and product strategies.

A few companies call the organization that sells the products a marketing organization. This is a misnomer and is confusing at the least. The organization that sells the products should only be called the selling organization.

From a leadership point of view, I believe true leaders must have a marketing sense and drive the people they lead with a marketing flair. Even if you're in a technical, mechanical, administrative or legal job, you should drive the people you lead with a marketing flair. Remember, these departments are the suppliers to product marketing. A great company, organization or group is one where every true team leader has a marketing orientation.

I believe United States companies should take the same leadership approach as Japanese companies. In Japan, many companies require all senior leaders of different departments to spend at least one year in marketing. Spending some time in marketing will enhance your presence.

Creates A Workable Culture And A Productive And Fun Environment

Culture

Culture is a word used many times in business. Each company likes to think it creates a culture. Employees talk about the culture of the company. Companies can go through cultural changes. Many times that happens when the head of the company is replaced with someone who has a different cultural bent. Sometimes the Board of a company replaces the CEO because they want a change in the culture of the company.

Three of the companies I worked for had the following culture:

- **Machine Accounting Company**, a very small data processing service company whose customers were small businesses.

Machine Accounting Company had no culture. Everyone worked like dogs. Everybody was paid bupkas. The owner had his mother wash the cement floor every other Sunday. There were air conditioners in two of the three small windows — none of which worked. I assumed the owner thought just seeing them would make us feel cooler during the Philadelphia 90 degree high humidity summers.

IBM made the owner build a structure around one of the first data processing computers — the 1401. To get the 1401 to work the room had to be no hotter than 75 degrees. In the summer we all fought each other over the projects that required the 1401. The problem was that going back and forth from 75 degrees to 90 degrees gave us all stiff necks.

There were no parties, no team building sessions, no group activities, no one on ones, no employee attitude surveys, no performance appraisals and no fun. It was all about the work. If the work got done, you were paid. If it didn't, you were fired.

- **Scientific Data Systems (SDS)** was a manufacturer of scientific and data processing computer equipment who had gross revenue of ninety five million dollars.

SDS was an aggressive small computer company fighting to stay alive and grow in a market dominated by companies like HP and IBM. We had to fight for every sale. We had to develop a niche where we could dominate and obtain name recognition.

Our culture was a company that was smarter, more creative, faster on its feet, a can do attitude and easier to do business with than our competitors. It was fun to work for this company. You had to learn on the job. You wanted to work hard and produce because you could see the effect of your contribution. When we beat out IBM or HP on a sale everyone in the company knew about it.

Although SDS gave its employees shares of stock, stock growth and stock bonuses were not our primary motivation. Our motivation was company success, David beating Goliath — company pride.

That all changed when Xerox purchased SDS in January 1969.

- **Xerox Corporation**

In a word the Xerox company culture was "political." There were some very smart, creative and hard working people at Xerox, but they were the exception not the rule. The SDS employees who were acquired by Xerox fought the political system the best we could, but we lost. The way to get ahead was to be good at playing politics. Almost everyone was in "cover your ass" mode. They were the ultimate Teflon suits — don't make any decision alone so nothing bad will stick to you.

Xerox's culture was don't rock the boat. Why stick your neck out — you won't get rewarded. If you fail you will be on the shit list. Make sure many managers and executives sign off on projects so if things don't go as planned you can say, "Well, they all agreed to do it." People in the company thought, "We are Xerox and therefore you should be happy to buy from us. I know it breaks a lot, but you're getting your product from the biggest in the industry."

Xerox's culture worked most of the time for Xerox copier products, but that attitude never worked for the SDS division. Xerox's solution was to rename us Xerox Data Systems — XDS. It didn't work. In a few years Xerox went out of the computer business.

Xerox developed and was committed to training their managers on leadership. I went to all the classes and learned a lot. Some of the information I am communicating to you in this book originated from those courses. However, after weeks of training, we all went back into the corporate culture. I guess you can't train culture. It's an attitude that has to emanate from the top and go down. I left Xerox many years ago. New management is running the company. I hope for the employee's sake the company's culture has changed.

I chose those three companies to give you an idea of a few different corporate cultures. The other companies I have worked for fall into one of these cultural ranges. For example, much later in my career, I worked for Infonet Services Corporation (ISC). ISC had a "can do" culture much like SDS. However, after my eleventh year, ISC was purchased by British Telecom Corporation (BT), a multibillion dollar British telecommunication company. Two years later I couldn't take the Xerox like culture of BT and I left.

A true leader can't allow the corporate culture to dictate how they lead their group. Just because the culture of the company sucks doesn't mean the group you lead has to suffer. You can create a different culture within the company's culture.

When I was a manager at Xerox, I did everything I could to make my team productive. I made decisions. When something needed to be expedited, I didn't make my people get all of the required management sign-offs. Those extra sign-offs didn't make for better decision making — it only slowed the decision down. If things didn't go as planned I was willing to take the heat from senior management. My team appreciated our department's culture because it was very different from the corporate culture. We were more productive. We had some fun. Except for my team and a few others, Xerox was slow to produce and very slow to create. Most of the Xerox employees were not having fun.

On the outside, the company's senior management had presence. It's easier to have presence when you run a multibillion dollar corporation. However, inside the company those same leaders were not viewed as people with presence because of the culture they either created or accepted.

Productive Environment

Management's responsibility is to create an environment in the workplace so that employees can be productive. People have more fun when they believe they are productive.

The things leaders can do to create a productive environment are:

- Give people time to perform their tasks. Pushing people to do more and more could be non-productive. People need a sense of accomplishment. Having too many tasks might put them in a situation where they feel they will never get any one of their tasks completed on time. If a person feels overburdened their reaction might be to slow down instead of speed up.

- Give people tasks they have the skills to perform. Challenging an employee is a good thing. However, a leader has to know the line that separates a challenging task from one that a specific person will not be able to complete successfully on time and with excellent quality.

- Productivity can be enhanced or diminished by the physical environment. Today we work in a cube environment. Cubes save space — space is money. Business cubes are a necessary evil. The design of the cube, the equipment, the tools and the facilities of the cube is the choice of the group leader. A good quality phone headset and a comfortable chair might be all that is necessary to make an employee more productive.

- The group leader must be sensitive to each employee's needs. We are all different. A file cabinet on the right works better for one employee where that same file cabinet works better on the left for another. A true leader will talk to the employee to find out what physical changes to their cube will make them more productive. Talking is not always enough. The leader should spend time watching how each employee works and then discuss physical changes with them.

Fun Environment

Creating an environment where people can be creative, decisive and happy will improve their productivity. People that like what they do are more productive. People who can have fun doing their job are more productive. Positive energy creates more productivity — negative energy creates less productivity.

The most effective leaders are the ones who know how to have fun. An unhappy leader is not going to create a fun environment. The unhappy leader will have more problems getting production from the team as compared to the happy leader. An unhappy leader doesn't have a positive presence. They have a negative presence.

A leader needs to be confident to show happiness. Some managers think they have to be serious all the time or the group they lead will not take them seriously. That point of view will result in less productivity and IS NOT TRUE.

Managers sometimes have to break the ice and tell a joke, burst out laughing (hopefully at something funny), Dress up on Halloween or just let others see them looking stupid. I'm not saying great leaders are jokesters. I am saying laughing is a real biochemical release from tension and stress.

People are attracted to those who are having a good time and know how to have fun. The serious boss who every once in awhile displays a great sense of humor, is very attractive to the people they lead.

A leader who has that kind of presence will generate many followers. Leaders with many happy followers are the most productive leaders.

Doesn't Hide Behind the Process

I despise managers who create processes so that no one individual has to take ownership or leadership. A business process where many people have to inspect and sign off on a project before it either gets started or completed enables people to hide behind the process.

"It's not my fault the project is late. I wasn't able to get all the sign-offs." "The process says I can't decide to go forward on this task before everyone agrees." "I don't care if the market is passing us by we can't ship this product until three Vice Presidents sign the launch document." "I'm not going to suggest a restaurant until we find out what the Gordon's want to eat." I call these people the Teflon suits. They don't have to take ownership because they created an environment where accountability is not encouraged.

The people who create these processes will never become true leaders. The people who accept these processes and use them to avoid accountability will never be viewed as someone with presence.

Leaders with presence don't hide behind anything. They show their presence by standing tall against policies that make it difficult to get things done. They show their presence and leadership by "tilting at windmills" instead of doing what is politically correct.

Accountability

Leaders have to hold their people accountable. Mister nice guy won't cut it. "I don't want to hold you accountable because you might not like me," will not cut it. Your people have a mission to accomplish. They have to be accountable for their tasks. In some cases they have to be accountable for the mission of the team. We are all in this together is the true leader's mantra.

Accountability without consequences is meaningless. A strong leader will be able to deal out the appropriate consequences for the individual's failure. Sometimes those consequences will be harsh and sometimes they will be mild. The leader must decide. What is critical is that each person is treated fairly. The team should know what to expect if they fail. The team needs to see that the person who failed received some form of punishment.

The leader also has to have the will to remove someone from the team should that person continue to not take responsibility for their actions. This is very difficult when that person is one of the most capable individual on the team. If the leader doesn't have the resolve to remove the best person the inmates will begin to run the asylum.

"OK, don't give me that fun crap, get the job done." Sounds harsh, but in the final analysis, this is the leader's responsibility. As the author of this book, I get to speak out of both sides of my mouth. In this case, I don't believe I'm being two faced.

Fun and being accountable don't have to be mutually exclusive. I feel just the opposite. When you're accountable, when you take ownership, when you stand up and say, "This is my responsibility," you assume more pressure which can lead to more stress. However, when you and the team complete the tasks, the sense of accomplishment and the sense of delivering on what you said you would deliver, is thrilling. Thrilling is a very fun emotion.

Promotes Teamwork

Every individual on a team is different mentally, physically, emotionally, creatively, skillfully and financially. It's the leader's job to know each individual member of the team to the degree that when working together, the team will reach the desired objective.

Understanding the team's bell shape curve is critical when a leader has the choice of who he or she hires. Except for a few specific situations, the left side of the bell shaped curve should be made up of people who are less experienced, younger mentally and emotionally. The curve then moves along the arch in experience, maturity and skill.

I don't want you to think I'm saying that young people are at one end and older people are at the opposite end of the curve. Experience and maturity should be more important to the leader than age.

Why do I think this mix of people make the best teams? Having many years in building and managing teams I have learned that highly skilled experienced people get set on a solution and have a problem changing their minds. Less experienced people aren't sure of the right solution and ask a lot of questions. The clash of egos happens less often with the optimal bell shaped curve than a team that has all the members at the right or left side of the curve.

It is possible for a team to be made up of mostly bright, highly experienced people who work together exceptionally well. I had such a team in my operations job at British Telecom. We were the fourth level of support. If no one else in the company could solve the customer's multimedia problem they called us. Knowledge, experience and the intelligence to find solutions by all the team members, was mandatory in getting the job done. Therefore, the team had to be made up of people who fit on the right side of the bell shaped curve.

I believe there was good judgment and good leadership on my part and the teams' part in making this work. The team I inherited worked out of countries in three different time zones. Therefore, the team realized the only way to get the job done was to work together. The new people I hired were all interviewed by the entire team to help me decide if they had the right skills, experience and most importantly a strong teamwork attitude. We spent months finding the right people. Knowing that hiring good people is a 50-50 proposition, I was fortunate that all the new team members worked out as planned.

When a leader inherits a team, the first priority is to observe how the team functions. If the team works well together, my philosophy is to leave a good thing alone. If the team is dysfunctional, the leader has to decide if he or she can manage and lead them into a cohesive and supportive group or make changes.

Those changes come in many forms. One, accept the team as is and when additional people are approved, hire ones who will round out the team and help others to fit in better. Two, get jobs outside of the organization for those team members that have talent, but don't fit the team's dynamics. Three, let go of the team members that are the main cause of the teamwork problem.

You might read the last paragraph and say "DUH!" However, if you have not done so before, it's no easy task. Many leaders find it hard to hire the right people. Many leaders find it hard to convince other departments to take their people. It has to be a win — win for both organizations. Lastly, a great many leaders find it hard to fire people especially if they have talent, but refuse to be a good team member.

From the beginning the leader should make it clear that supporting, communicating and caring about every team member is *mandatory*. The leader must insist that if conflicts between team members happen they are to be brought to him or her to handle the situation. That will require trust that their leader will be fair to all and make decisions that favor the company, the team and the task. The team members have to trust their leader will not make a decision on the situation that favors any specific team member because he likes them better.

Some leaders use a team counsel method to resolve conflicts. With the right mix of team members it can be a very effective teamwork tool. In the counsel approach, the issue is brought up to the entire team for them to decide right and wrong. The leader acts as the moderator and only if necessary, the final decision maker. Sometimes the best way to get the message across to certain members is by having their peers give their opinion.

I'm not a big fan of *mandatory* team building events. Team dinners, paint ball games, team picnics and other unique events are short lived once the team gets back to their daily jobs and has to deal with each other. The best team building events are the ones that the team decides would be fun and convinces the team leader to fund the event. I have never refused to fund and participate in a team generated event. On the other hand, I have been forced by senior management or the human resources department to hold mandatory team building events because *they* believed it would somehow create a better teamwork situation.

The employees had fun at the mandatory event and enjoyed the time off, but did it create a day to day closer and happier team — USUALLY NOT! Happy teams come from the leadership they receive on a daily basis.

The goal of a leader is to get the job done, maximize the capabilities of each team member and have fun in the process. Cooperative team dynamics is critical to achieve that goal. Without that productivity will suffer, the job performance will suffer and the team, including the leader, will not be having fun.

Empowers Employees

The best way to create happier and more productive employees is by empowerment. When they feel responsible for their performance they usually don't blame others for their mistakes or lack of performance. This limits conflicts, egos and team malcontents. It does have a downside in that the empowered employee might fight harder defending their position. The bottom line is whether or not the job got done. If not, the empowered employee doesn't have a strong defense.

The leader always has to evaluate each team member as to their desire to be empowered. Some members don't want the stress of being empowered. They usually have a problem with self confidence and believe they will fail if empowered. I prefer confident employees, but in a bell shaped curved team that's not always possible.

When dealing with a less confident team member, the leader must still insist the employee take on the task. The leader should offer their total support in making sure the team member will be successful. However, he has to be careful not to do the task for the employee. The leader should help him or her from the background so the team member feels they played a big part in the accomplishment of the task.

For example, when the employee asks, "What should I do" the leader should say, "If you were completely on your own what decision would you make?" The end result should be the employee has a sense of accomplishment once the task is complete. The more tasks he or she feels that sense of accomplishment the sooner they will become more self-confident. Once self-confident they will no longer need the leader to help them.

Makes It Easy To Be Replaced

Become easy to replace — are you kidding? What leader, who has worked hard for many years, would want to take specific actions to become easily replaced? The answer is the true leader with a strong presence.

True leaders are confident people. They're secure in their position within the company or group. True leaders understand that having a potential leader on their team will enable them to run their organization from a higher level. That means making the critical decisions while the potential leader deals with the less critical ones. They realize the team needs a "go to person" when they are out sick, on vacation or just not available. True leaders believe they are able to grow to a higher position only if they can leave their current team to a qualified and respected leader.

To become easy to replace you have to find a person within your group who has many of the leadership traits stated above. Explain to that person they will not receive a promotion and a new title. If they are capable of becoming a true leader, they will prove they can be the "go to" person without the title. Make it clear they will have to perform their day to day job while having to perform extra work as a leader. Inform that person you're going to tell the team and other group managers that you will be giving him or her some leadership responsibilities.

If you can find such a person, sit her down and ask if she wants to take a leadership position within the group. If she says no, accept her decision. Don't question it. Don't try to change her mind. Make it clear that your relationship with her is not affected by turning the offer down. There is no penalty in saying no. I have the deepest respect for a person that knows themselves and puts their personal happiness in front of a potential promotion.

If the person says yes, ask them why. If their answer comes across as wanting power, money or ego, tell them they would not be a good fit. If their answer comes across as wanting to learn and grow as a leader or wanting to make a difference as a leader, let them know that they will be given every opportunity to succeed.

Now the burden of leadership falls on both of you. You will have to commit yourself to helping that person lead. That means giving up some of your authority and letting them make decisions on their own. It means you will help them learn from their mistakes and not punish them for making those mistakes. It means letting them run a project with some team members, without your interference. It means letting them represent you and the team at certain managers meetings without you being there.

Over my career as a leader I have had the good fortune to be able to teach and grow leaders that have had great success replacing me.

If you don't have a candidate within your group you have two choices. Do nothing and let management deal with the problem after you move on. I hate this option. You will have to be available all the time, the team will be without trusted guidance and the company will not be served by you moving on.

Second choice is to make your next hire a person who has the ability to do the job for which you're hiring plus learn and grow to be a leader.

Finding such a person will not be an easy task. Usually a person who wants to be a leader is looking for a leadership job — not a job that has that responsibility without the title. This might force you to hire a less senior person who would love the opportunity to grow as a leader.

If you're forced to take that path, you and the new hire will have to work extra hard convincing the team and others managers there is a leader underneath this inexperienced skin. To minimize the stress on both of you I would not announce the new hire as a potential leader. He or she has a job to do and needs to prove they can do it before they will have a chance to get any respect. If they are the right person, the team will recognize they have the *presence* to be a leader before you announce you're grooming him or her as a leader. I have done this with success.

If you're a college student with a goal to get into executive management you need to develop presence. If you're a person working for a company, group or organization and want to become the leader, you need to develop presence. If you're a current leader, but feel you need something to enhance your leadership position, all of the building blocks above are necessary to obtain that goal. Don't ignore any of them.

Enjoy the journey — you deserve it.